Physical Sciences:
A Primary Teacher's Guide

Kevin Carlton
and
Eric Parkinson

CASSELL

Cassell
Villiers House
41/47 Strand
London
WC2N 5JE

387 Park Avenue South
New York
NY 10016-8810

British Library Cataloguing-in-Publication Data
A catalogue record for this book is available from the British Library.

ISBN: 0–304–32766–2

Typeset by Litho Link Ltd, Welshpool, Powys, Wales

Printed and bound in Great Britain by Redwood books, Trowbridge, Wiltshire

PHYSICAL SCIENCES: A PRIMARY TEACHER'S GUIDE

Also available in the Cassell Education series:

Contents

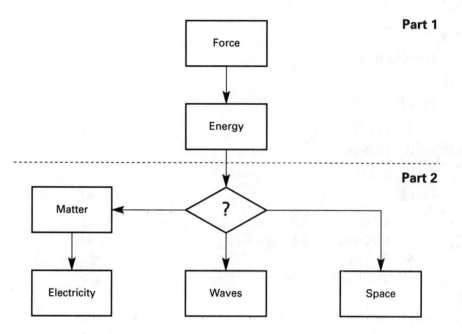

Part 1

Part 2

Introduction

Welcome to the world of physical science. For many of you this may be your first encounter with this fascinating domain. To you we extend a particular welcome.

Traditionally, the physical sciences have been dominated by a mathematical approach. This book attempts to remedy this serious error. Quite simply, we believe that physics minus maths *is* possible!

To make the physical sciences more accessible to the educated beginner, we have focused our attention on areas like 'Force', 'Energy' and 'Waves'. We believe that it is through consideration of these fundamental concepts that enjoyment of the journey towards an understanding of the way the universe works can begin. And this way, you will end up with a firm grasp of the main ideas underpinning the enormously interesting world of the physical scientist.

Knowledge and understanding depend upon an ability to see the whole picture and the skill to transfer this knowledge to new contexts. Clearly, a book designed to accomplish this aim requires some structure. To help you on your journey of understanding we have devised the 'route map' shown opposite.

Part 1 contains two core topics of a conceptual nature: 'Force' and 'Energy'. These topics permeate the rest of the book. In order to understand any topics in Part 2, it is essential to have read Part 1 first!

Part 2 contains material of a more concrete nature upon which to hang the concepts of Part 1. It covers the real world with topics like 'Waves' and 'Space'. There is also some structure to Part 2. If you want to know about 'Space', you can move directly to this topic. If you want to know more about 'Electricity', you first need to understand the nature of 'Matter' itself. The route map should make this clear. *Bon voyage!*

We would like to acknowledge the help of John Bexon, who helped with the chapter on matter, and all the INSET students/teachers who provided helpful comments.

Kevin Carlton and Eric Parkinson

Part 1

Chapter 1

Force

INTRODUCTION

What does the word 'force' mean to you? No doubt you will have used the word in non-scientific ways. If we look at the way we commonly use 'force', we may find clues to the way the word is used by scientists. Let's look at some examples.

We quite often refer to 'force' when talking about the armed forces. As their name suggests, these people are there to enforce law and order. In other words, their job is to impose the will of their political masters.

Let's take another example, this time from schools. A teacher may refer to the need to force some children to carry out certain tasks. What we mean here is that some form of compulsion is employed.

We have all met 'forceful personalities', you know, the ones who always get their own way at meetings. Such people are able to dominate others.

These are only three examples of the way the word 'force' is commonly used. There are, of course, quite a few more – like the way we talk about 'social' or 'economic forces'. Many of these may be *borrowed* from science. **However, care is needed to identify those which are actually scientific.**

You will see, in most of the examples that you can think of, that the word 'force' usually refers to causing things to happen or to change. To force something is to make something happen which would not do so on its own. In everyday language we could say that **a force causes things to happen or change**.

THE EFFECTS OF A FORCE – OR SCIENCE IN THE SUPERMARKET

We can find examples of forces at work in every aspect of our lives. Even a mundane shopping trip can help in our understanding of fundamental scientific concepts . . .

LUCY MADDISON

Imagine you are in the supermarket. You have just found a trolley and grasped the handle. The trolley does not move on its own. You need to push it towards the aisle in order to do your shopping. What is going on here? You have just pushed the trolley, and the effect of this push is to move the trolley. It was stationary, but now it is moving. A change has occurred as a result of you applying a force to the handle of the trolley.

☐   **A force can have the effect of making a stationary object begin to move.**

So far so good. As you proceed along the aisle (at a steady pace), you notice a particularly interesting item on the shelf. You stop to take a closer look. Do you let go of the trolley? Not likely! There was quite a queue to obtain it in the first place and you are not going to give it up. Instead you hang on to the trolley handle.

A strange thing happens. You have stopped, but the trolley seems to disagree and wants to carry on moving! (All supermarket trolleys have minds of their own, don't they?) You have to pull on the handle of the trolley to get it to come to rest. Another change has occurred as a result of you applying a force to the handle of the trolley.

☐   **A force can have the effect of making a moving object stop.**

You put the item in your trolley and off you go again. Soon you arrive at the end of the aisle. What do you do next? Heave on the handle to try and make the trolley turn around the corner and into the next aisle. All that heaving has done the trick and reluctantly the trolley obeys. You have managed to bring about yet another change. This time the trolley has not stopped or started, but it has changed direction.

☐   **A force can have the effect of making a moving object change direction.**

As you progress down the new aisle, you notice that your favourite drink is on special offer but there is only one left. If you are not quick enough, you may miss out! You push harder on the handle of your trolley and you are really moving along now. The items on the shelves are just a blur as you speed by. All this extra effort has caused another change. The trolley has started to move faster.

☐   **A force can have the effect of making a moving object move faster.**

Oh, bad luck! Before you could get there someone has beaten you to it. You have no need to hurry any more: after all, you might cause an accident as you did not realize you were going quite so fast. You had better slow down a bit. How do you do this? Why, you pull on the handle, of course. This causes the trolley to change speed again, but this time it is slowing down.

☐   **A force can have the effect of making a moving object slow down.**

This is not an exhaustive list of things that a force can do. We will look into this in more detail later on. It would be useful here to summarize what we have discovered by thinking about what effects a force can have.

All the examples so far have been associated with movement. The movement of the trolley has been affected by applying a force to the handle. When a body is moving in a straight line at an even pace, it is said to have a constant **velocity**.

A common misconception

In everyday experience things do not keep moving on their own. If you let go of a moving supermarket trolley, it will soon come to rest. This experience leads many people to conclude that **moving objects will come to rest unless there is a force present to keep them moving**. This would mean that a force would have the effect of stopping a change from happening. This goes against what has been said so far.

REPRESENTING A FORCE

A force is a different type of quantity from, say, volume. With volume all you need to say about it is how big it is. You are only concerned with size.

With a force you need to say more. You need to talk not only about the size but also about the direction in which the force acts. For this reason, in diagrams we usually represent a force by an arrow.

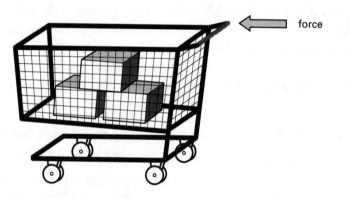

force

The direction of the arrow represents the direction of the force, and the length of the arrow tells us about the strength of the force. Double the length of arrow means double the force.

> **Do not confuse these arrows, which represent forces, with arrows which represent directions of motion. The direction of movement and the direction of a force acting need not be the same.**

Remember, when you forced the supermarket trolley to slow down, you applied a force backwards as the trolley moved forwards. You pulled back on the handle and the trolley slowed down.

backward force
on handle

forward motion
of trolley

MORE THAN ONE FORCE – A BALANCING ACT

Up until now we have been discussing the effects of *a* force. Life is seldom that simple. Usually there are a *number* of forces acting on a single body. To understand what is going on in everyday situations we really need to consider what happens when many forces act together on one body.

Let us change the scene from all this rushing around with shopping trolleys to something more tranquil. Think about a vase on a table. In scientific terms we refer to the vase as a 'body'. Ask yourself if there are any forces acting on this body. You might be tempted to say that there are not, particularly if you consider what has been said about the effects of a force.

Remember, one of the effects of a force is to make things move. Is there any evidence of this with the vase? No, it just stays where it is. Another effect of a force is to make things stop. But the vase is not moving, it just sits there. What about making things change direction? Is there a force causing this to happen? No, the vase just stays right where it is. Is there an effect causing the vase to go faster or to go more slowly? Once again the answer is no. The only possible conclusion from these observations is that there is no force involved.

But there *is* a force involved, you know! Take away the table that the vase is standing on and see what happens. The vase crashes to the floor. Ah, we have forgotten about gravity. Clearly, a force is pulling the vase downwards even when it is just sitting on our table.

So there is a force acting: a downward force. Gravity is always there, pulling the flowers downwards. There must be another force acting upwards to balance the effect of the downward force of gravity – otherwise the vase would get pulled through the table! The table is exerting an upward force on the vase, which has the effect of counteracting the downward force of gravity.

There is no longer a problem once you realize that there is *more than one force involved*, and in some way the effects of the forces are able to cancel each other out.

> **When there are two forces acting equally in opposite directions on a body, their effects cancel each other out. We say that the two forces balance.**

That is why in the first section we were at pains to ensure that we talked about a force and not *forces*.

Let us leave the stationary vase and go back to the supermarket. What about our moving trolley? Now we know that there is gravity acting downwards and a reaction at the floor. These have effects which balance, just as in the case of the flowers.

The trolley is also moving across the floor. It is common experience that if we do not keep pushing on that handle, the trolley will soon come to rest. We need to keep pushing just to keep it moving. How can that be? If we stop pushing and the trolley starts to slow down, there must be a force acting to slow down the trolley. This force is the force of **friction**. What we are doing when we push on the handle to keep the trolley moving is exerting a force *equal* to that of friction *but in the opposite direction*. If we push too hard, the trolley speeds up; if we do not push hard enough, it will begin to slow down. Only when we *exactly balance* the force of friction do we enable the trolley to continue at constant speed.

Balanced forces appear all over the place, and a good thing that is too! Think of the times when things have gone wrong and you have wished the ground to give way and swallow you up . . .

ABOUT THE NATURE OF FORCE

We started off this chapter by analysing how we used the word 'force'. We followed this up by looking at examples of what a force can do. We now have a pretty good idea of what a force or a number of forces can do. What we have not really attempted to answer is the question of what exactly a force *is*. It is to that question that we now address ourselves.

Back to the supermarket

Let's return to our good friend, the supermarket trolley. What exactly is going on here? Quite simply you, the shopper, are pushing and pulling at the handle of the trolley. The result of all this heaving and tugging is that the trolley is 'forced' to obey your wishes (as if!) and move around the supermarket under your control. So far we have only considered what has happened to the trolley. The trolley, though, is only half the story. We have not considered the person who is doing all the pushing and shoving. Don't feel left out, because now we are going to consider you, the hard-pressed shopper.

The point is that, left to itself, the trolley will not do anything. It is only when it is acted upon by the shopper that a change occurs. In fact, what has happened is that the shopper and the trolley have come together and an **interaction** has taken place. How do the two interact? The answer to this fundamental question is that they interact *through a force*.

> **A very useful way of looking at the nature of force is to consider it as an interaction between two bodies.**

This interaction is by no means one-sided. If you consider how you feel when you have finished your shopping you will realize that all that pushing and pulling wears you out. How nice it would be if you had a helper to manoeuvre the trolley on your behalf. The pushing of the trolley does have an effect on you!

To understand fully the *interactiveness* of force, we need on each occasion to consider the two bodies which are interacting. In the case of the supermarket trolley, these two bodies are the pusher (you, the shopper) and the pushed (the trolley itself).

Oh no, not supermarket trolleys again!

Imagine the scene in a supermarket. Two naughty children have gone to the toy department and each has got a giant horseshoe magnet and placed it in their trolley. What happens when the children let the trolleys go? (See illustration on page 10.)

Ask yourself, 'Is there a force acting?' There surely is. Those magnets are extremely strong, you know! Of course, each of the trolleys will start to move and will tend to speed up while it is moving. Each trolley experiences a force.

Another way of looking at this situation is to consider that the two trolleys are interacting with one another. After all, if one trolley were there alone, nothing would happen, would it? Think about each of the trolleys. The first trolley is attracted towards the second one. *But* . . . the second trolley is also attracted to the first. The force which each trolley experiences is only *half* of the total interaction.

A common misconception

> **It is vitally important that the *interactive nature* of force is not confused with *balancing forces*.**

Each trolley in the previous example will experience the same-size force but in the opposite direction. This must not be confused with balancing forces.

In the case of balancing forces, there are two different but equal and opposite forces which act on the *same body*.

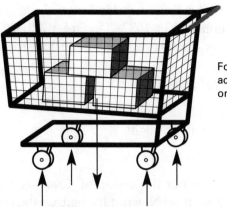

Force of gravity
acts downwards
on the trolley.

Floor pushes up on the wheels of the trolley.

In the case of the interactive nature of a force, two *different bodies* experience different sides of the effect of the one force.

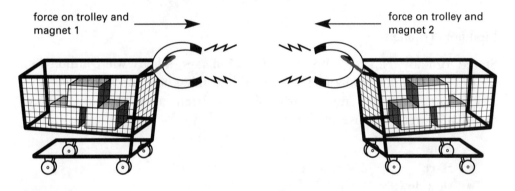

force on trolley and
magnet 1

force on trolley and
magnet 2

Remember . . .

This works as well for pushing forces as for pulling forces. It could easily have been that the two trolleys above were connected by a compressed spring. This would have the effect of making the trolleys repel each other, and they would then experience forces pushing them apart instead of pulling them together.

> **When dealing with a force, look out for the two bodies which are interacting. There are always two bodies involved.**

NEWTON – MORE FORMALLY

The unit of force is the **newton** and this is named after the great man himself.

Sir Isaac Newton (1642–1727) is often referred to as the father of modern physics. Certainly his thinking has had a marked effect on the way that physics is conducted, an effect which has lasted up to the present day. Newton's major work, entitled *Philosophiae Naturalis Principia Mathematica*, is still world renowned, even though it was published in 1687. The great Albert Einstein accepted that in order to make his famous discoveries he had to 'stand on Newton's shoulders'.

A favourite quote about Newton goes as follows:

> Nature and Nature's laws lay hid in Night!
> God said, *Let Newton be!* and all was light.

Alexander Pope

What is of particular interest to us in our discussion of 'force' is a group of sayings known as **Newton's laws of motion**. Newton formalized the concept of force and motion that we have been thinking about so far. As we progress, you will see that the ideas he developed look remarkably like concepts that we have already discussed. Careful consideration of Newton's laws will extend the force concept still further. Let's take these laws in order.

First law of motion

Stated formally, Newton's first law of motion says: **a body will continue in a state of rest or uniform motion in a straight line unless acted upon by a force.**

This single sentence sums up what we have been saying to date. We have said that **a force** can cause an object to:

- **stop**
- **start**
- **slow down**
- **speed up**
- **change direction**

If you think about it, each of the changes mentioned above can be summarized as causing a body no longer to 'continue in a state of rest or uniform motion in a straight line'. After all, if it *stops*, it has ceased moving; if it *starts*, it is no longer in a state of rest; if it *slows down* or *speeds up*, its motion is no longer uniform; if it *changes direction*, it is no longer moving in a straight line.

Newton considered all these things and expressed them formally as his first law. *Remember*, this idea goes against common experience. It is common experience that, unless you apply a force to an object, it will *not* keep moving; rather it will come to rest.

This is because it is quite difficult on Earth to get away from forces. There is always gravity and there is nearly always friction. Why does your supermarket trolley gradually slow down when you stop pushing it? After all, this is not what Newton's law tells us should be happening – or is it? Newton's law refers to what *a force* will do. The force of gravity and/or friction must be considered in the case of your gradually slowing trolley. In the absence of such forces – in outer space, say – the trolley would carry on for ever at the same speed and in a straight line: in other words, it would carry on at the same velocity.

When you apply a force to *counterbalance* these other forces, you can see Newton's law working. So you push the trolley to make it carry on at a steady speed in a straight line. This is possible because instead of the trolley being acted upon by no force, it is acted upon by a number of forces which *balance*. The floor pushes up on the trolley to balance gravity, and your push cancels out friction. The net result is that it behaves as though there were no force there at all.

If you consider examples like spacecraft moving in space, where there is no air to cause resistance, Newton's point of view makes more sense. Spacecraft that visit planets of the solar system do not need to keep their rocket motors running all the time during the flight. The only time the motors are needed is to make minor adjustments to the course to keep the craft on target.

Although friction is just about zero in space, there is still the effect of gravity. So the path taken by spacecraft in the solar system will be curved and not straight. The point is that friction does not slow them down.

The genius of people like Newton is to see beyond everyday experience and perceive the underlying principles.

Second law of motion

Newton's second law may be stated in a number of different ways. The formal statements of the law tend to be a bit mathematical, so we will think about the concept first and then conclude by putting together our own version.

The reason that Newton's second law is expressed in mathematical terms is that it is involved in asking the question, 'How much?' How much force is needed to stop the moving trolley, and how long will it take? What effect does the amount of shopping in the trolley have on the required force?

First of all, let's think about the effect of the amount of shopping in the trolley. It is clear from our everyday experience of these fiendish devices that, as we go round the supermarket filling our trolleys with shopping, they become more difficult to control.

Think about the case where two perfectly matched shoppers have identical trolleys. The first shopper has an empty trolley; the second shopper has a heavily laden trolley. The manager of the supermarket has programmed the trolleys to have a certain maximum speed. If the two shoppers start together and push the two trolleys with equal force, which trolley will reach the maximum speed first? The answer is, of course, the empty trolley.

☐ **The more heavily laden the trolley, the longer it takes to reach maximum speed given the same push.**

Imagine that you have been shopping for some time. Your trolley is getting quite full. You meet a friend who has just arrived and so has an empty trolley. You have not seen each other for months and there is a lot of news to swap. You find that if you want to keep up with your friend, as he stops and starts, you need to push and pull at the trolley much harder than he does.

☐ **The more heavily laden your trolley, the harder you have to push to keep up.**

Scientists would say that the more heavily laden a trolley is, the greater is its mass. The last two statements in **bold** explain the effect of the mass of the trolley.

Now think about two identical trolleys. They have the same amount of shopping in each, so they have the same mass. This time we have two different shoppers. One works out at the local gym and is very strong. The other is a heavy smoker who never takes any exercise and is much weaker. In a race to reach maximum speed, the shopper who is able to push his trolley the hardest will always win.

☐ **The harder you push your trolley, the less time it takes to get to maximum speed.**

To a scientist, a body which is picking up speed is accelerating. The quicker it reaches the maximum speed, the greater is the acceleration.

We are now in a position to be able to make up our own version of Newton's second law. It says that **for a stated mass, the larger the force you apply, the greater will be the acceleration; for a larger mass, a larger force is needed to produce the same acceleration as for a smaller mass.**

But wait a minute! What about when you push something – say, a car with its handbrake on – and it refuses to move? Does this law still apply? Think about *why* it refuses to move. The answer is because there is another force, perhaps friction, acting to stop it. Your push and the restricting force balance one another and the net force is *zero*.

It is logical to expect the acceleration to be zero in this case, and this means that the car does not move. This is what the law predicts if zero force acts. An object will only accelerate, or be caused to move, if an *unbalanced* force acts upon it.

Third law of motion

Newton's third law is bound up with the nature of force. Let's leave the world of the supermarket for a while. In fact, let's leave the world itself and head off into space . . . deep, deep space . . . Here we can consider forces in an uncluttered environment, free of messy gravity and an atmosphere with all the complexities of air resistance.

We are in a spaceship. We are heading off to a distant galaxy. Our rocket engine is pouring gases out of the back and we are travelling faster and faster. But how? When we exert a force on Earth, we usually have something (the Earth) to push against. Suppose you leap in the air. You push against the Earth and the Earth pushes against you. The rocket, however, has nothing to push against!

An important question arises here. How can an object ever move if the two forces at either side of the interaction work equally strongly in two opposite directions?

The source of confusion arises in many people's minds because they consider that these two forces must balance if they are equal and opposite, and there can therefore never be any motion. The dilemma is resolved once it is realized that the two sides of the force in an interaction act on *different bodies*.

How does this apply to the supermarket trolley? Think about what would happen if you were wearing roller skates and pushed the trolley . . . One side of the interaction is that the trolley feels a force which causes it to start moving forwards. The other side of the interaction is that you feel a force pushing you in the opposite direction. If you are not holding on to the trolley, but only pushing it, then the trolley will go one way and you will go the other.

In the example from space, the rocket pushes against the hot gases and at the same time the hot gases push against the rocket. In the emptiness of space, with no matter, there are two bodies out there between which the interaction takes place. The rocket and the gases are considered to be the two bodies because each has mass.

The third law is currently the cause of some controversy. The way that it was originally formulated by Newton is considered liable to give rise to many misconceptions. Research has shown that even some professional physicists get it wrong!

We are not saying that the original formulation of the law is incorrect; only that it is easily misunderstood. A new formulation of the law has been suggested by C. Hellingman in an article in *Physics Education*, March 1992. He suggests the law could be expressed as: **'a force is one side of an interaction; the interaction takes place between two bodies, working equally strongly in the two opposite directions'**.

This reciprocal nature of forces has led some people to talk of forces always acting in pairs. As we will show, this is a potentially misleading point of view. The danger is that, instead of the situation being viewed in terms of two sides of a single interaction, the pair of forces are considered as two separate entities.

GRAVITY

Not only did Newton 'invent' or discover the laws of motion, he is also credited with discovering gravity. At first, that sounds a bit ridiculous. Surely it was known for centuries before Newton that if an apple growing on a tree became dislodged it would fall to the ground. Well, of course it was! It is not that for which Newton is given credit.

Think about Newton's third law again for a moment. If the apple in the tree falls, it is because there is a force acting upon it. We call this the force of gravity. We will look at that more closely later on. According to our statement about the third law, the force which attracts the apple to the ground is one side of an interaction. Between which two bodies does the interaction take place? One is obviously the apple itself. To where does the apple fall? The surface of the Earth. So the Earth is the other body involved. Again according to Newton's third law, the force acts equally strongly in the two opposite directions. This means that the apple attracts the Earth with a force equal, but of course opposite, to the force with which the Earth attracts the apple. However, the Earth is much larger than the apple and so the apple is perceived to move whereas the Earth is not.

The point is that gravity acts between any two bodies which have mass. Each body will attract the other with an equal force. The question which arises next is 'How strong is that force?'

Ask yourself which has more mass, an apple or an adult person. Naturally, the person has more mass. Think about the force of gravity which acts between the Earth and the apple. Now think about the force of gravity which acts between the Earth and the person. Which of the two is larger? The force of gravity between the Earth and the person, of course. (Incidentally, we can soon get tired of saying, 'the force of gravity between the Earth and something'. Instead we call this force the **weight** of the thing.) Newton realized this and decided that the weight of any body increases with its mass. In other words: **the greater the mass, the greater the weight.**

Mass and weight

One constant source of confusion for non-scientists is the problem of the difference between mass and weight. **Weight** is simply the force of gravity which holds a body to the Earth. The **mass** of the body is the quantity of matter in it. For example, if you went to a shop to buy some apples, you would ask for so many kilograms (or pounds in the UK) of apples. The greengrocer would then measure out the correct amount of apples, plus the usual 'little bit over, is that all right?'. What you have bought is a quantity of apples. So far, so good.

How does the shopkeeper measure out the amount of apples? In the good old days he would have used a balance. On one side of the balance is a pan in which known masses of metal are placed. On the other side of the balance, the shopkeeper puts the apples. What is going on here exactly? The answer is that the weight of the apples and the weight of the metal masses should be the same if the masses are equal. The balance is being used to compare weights and thereby compare masses. This process has come to be called 'weighing apples'. In common speech we now say that the apples 'weigh' 1 kilogram. What we really mean to say is that the apples have the same weight as a kilogram mass would have.

Of course, nowadays electronic scales find the weight of the apples by measuring the force of gravity on the apples. Then they work out what mass would cause such a force and give the shopkeeper a measure of the mass of the apples directly. They do not compare the weight with that of a known mass. That is where the source of confusion lies.

> The mass of apples is the quantity of apples you have and is measured in kilograms. The weight of the apples is the force of gravity between the Earth and the apples and is measured in newtons.

Gravity and other worlds . . .

If what we have been saying is true, there should be a force of gravity between any two bodies, even two apples. The reason that you have probably not noticed such a force is that gravity is really rather a weak force, and is not noticeable unless one of the masses is the size of at least a minor planet.

What about the force of gravity between the apple and the Moon? Yes, that is measurable. Gravity on the surface of the Moon is approximately one-sixth that of the gravity on the surface of the Earth. Remember the films of the astronauts 'walking' on the surface of the Moon?

You might be misled here though. You might think that the mass of the Moon is one-sixth that of the Earth. Unfortunately, you would be wrong. The force of gravity between two bodies depends not only upon their masses, but also on the distance between their centres. In fact, if you double the distance between the two bodies then you quarter the force of gravity. The Moon is much smaller than the Earth. That means that when you are standing on the surface of the Moon you are nearer to its centre than you are to the centre of the Earth when standing on the Earth's surface. The fact that you are closer to the centre of the Moon means that the force of gravity is stronger.

Just for fun, think about the shopkeeper on the Moon. Would the electronic scale and the balancing scale both give the correct reading on the Moon? The answer is that the old-fashioned balance would work perfectly well. The force of gravity between the Moon and the kilogram mass is the same as the force between the Moon and the kilogram of apples. The new-fangled electronic weighing machine would not give the correct answer though. It would still think it was on the Earth, and since it would be measuring the weight of the apples on the Moon, it would give the wrong reading. It would need adjusting to compensate for the lower gravity on the Moon.

FRICTION

According to Newton's first law of motion, a body such as a moving supermarket trolley will continue moving in a straight line at a steady speed unless it is acted upon by a force. It is common experience that, if left to themselves, moving supermarket trolleys do not carry on moving for ever. They very soon come to rest. As we have already discussed, there must be a force acting on the trolley. If you recall, we decided that the force was due to friction.

A force does not have to slow a moving object down; it can cause an object to start moving or to speed up. Friction is, after all, only one force. Can you think of any examples where friction causes a body to start moving or to speed up? No, of course not. We have just discovered one important property of the force of friction.

☐   **Friction always acts in such a direction as to *oppose* motion.**

The great friction debate

1. Friction is our enemy . . .

Friction is always to be found slowing us down. We take a lot of trouble to get our heavy trolley up to speed. Once we have done that, we cannot rest because we have to keep pushing to overcome friction.

What about our 'best friend' the motor car? Just think how we could economize on fuel if there were no friction! We need to run the engine in order to get our heavy car to reach the desired speed. The only reason we need to keep the engine going once we have reached that speed is because friction is acting against us. We need to keep the engine going to push against friction. Without friction we could simply turn off the engine once we had reached the right speed, and coast along on our merry way just like the spaceship cruising in deep space.

Yes, there is no doubt about it, friction is our enemy.

2. Friction is our friend . . .

It has to be admitted that friction slows you down. But just think for a minute about what life would be like without friction. Let's take a closer look at driving your car.

Imagine for a moment that you have managed to reach your desired speed. You are cruising along. Suddenly a ball bounces in the road in front of you. Look out, there is a child running after the ball! Quick, hit the brakes! What happens? Without friction nothing happens. The brakes work by rubbing a brake-shoe against a drum connected to the wheel. It is friction between the two that causes the wheel to slow down. The tyres of your car are now rubbing against the road. It is friction that causes the car to slow down.

Suppose you say that there is no need to slow down to avoid hitting the child in the road. All you need to do is swerve to avoid a collision. Think about that for a moment. To swerve means to change direction. According to Newton, you need a force in order to do this. You turn the steering-wheel and the wheels on the ground turn. The wheels are in contact with the ground and the force of friction acts between the two. This force causes you to change direction. If you doubt this, just think about making a sharp turn on an icy road and you will see how important friction is to steering!

It is beginning to look as if friction is important to us after all. Without it we cannot steer or stop. Actually, without it we would never have got started in the first place. It is the force of friction between the ground and the wheels that allows the car to move forwards. Yes, friction is definitely our friend.

You might get the impression that in the last example friction was *causing* motion and not *opposing* it. You think this because the car moved. The force of friction acts between the road and the wheel. Without friction the driving wheels would simply spin round and round. The force of friction opposes this spinning motion of the wheels. In other words, the force of friction opposes the *relative motion* of the road and the wheels. It might be better to say: **friction between two bodies always acts so as to oppose their relative motion.**

The friction acts between the road and the wheel. The motion that the friction opposes is the motion between the road and the wheel. It so happens that we have been clever enough to turn that to our advantage and get the car to move.

The only conclusion you can draw from the great friction debate is that sometimes friction is our friend and sometimes it is our enemy. Sometimes we wish to increase friction, as when we want extra grip from our tyres, and sometimes we wish to reduce friction, as when we want to allow the wheels of our trolley to turn freely. If we want to control friction, we need to know more about how it works.

How friction works

Friction occurs whenever two surfaces are in contact. They do not have to be moving. Think about the case of a car parked on a hill with the handbrake on. The car is not moving, but there is still a frictional force acting. It acts between the wheels and the ground to stop the car sliding down the hill, and it acts between the brakes and the road wheels to stop it rolling down the hill.

Naturally enough, friction that acts between things that are in relative motion is called **dynamic friction**, while friction that acts between things that are not moving relative to one another is called **static friction**. As a general rule, static friction is slightly stronger than dynamic friction.

In order for friction to work between two objects, there has to be a force pushing them together. Investigations have shown that, the stronger this force is, the greater is the force of friction between them. Just think about how much easier it is to keep an empty shopping trolley moving at constant speed than it is to keep a full one in motion. (We talk about moving at constant speed because the only force you need to apply here is the one needed to overcome friction. If we were to talk about accelerating the trolley, then the greater mass of the fuller trolley would mean that it required a greater force according to Newton's second law.)

But just how does friction work? When we think about two surfaces in contact, we usually imagine that they are touching all over the area of contact. A greatly magnified picture would show that this is not the case. Instead, the tiny roughnesses of both surfaces cause the actual points of contact to be both very small and very few. The force which is pushing the two surfaces together is acting on a rather small fraction of the overall area. If you like, the force is concentrated at a small number of points. The huge pressure (see the next section) involved here is sufficient to cause the material of the two objects to fuse, or weld, together at the points of contact. If you want to move the two objects relative to one another, you have to apply sufficient force to break apart these welds. This is the force of friction.

If we wish to increase friction, we need to design surfaces which will readily weld together. Generally this means we need to use rough surfaces. This reduces the number of points of contact between the objects and increases the pressure at each point. This in turn increases the likelihood of welding taking place. The other way we can increase friction is by pushing the two objects together more strongly. That is why squeezing the brakes of your car harder increases the braking force.

If we wish to reduce the force of friction, we have somehow to stop the welding process from happening. We can do this by introducing a third material, a liquid. The liquid gets between the two surfaces and fills in the valleys of the roughnesses. The force pushing the two objects together is partially transmitted by the liquid. This reduces the pressure at the points of contact and reduces the amount of welding that takes place. Such a liquid is called a **lubricant**. That is why we put oil in our engines, to reduce the friction between the moving parts. This not only makes our cars run more smoothly, but also reduces engine wear and prolongs the life of the car.

Non-solid friction

So far we have been discussing friction as if it applied only to solid objects in contact with solid objects. In fact there is a kind of friction that acts between fluids (liquids and gases are lumped together here as fluids). We do not actually call it friction, although its effects are much the same. We call it **viscosity**.

To get an idea of viscosity, consider water and treacle. Treacle has much more resistance to flowing than water. Just think about the difference between wading around in a bath of treacle and wading around in a bath of water. Treacle is more viscous than water. Sometimes non-scientists refer to treacle being 'thicker' than water. What they really mean is 'more viscous'.

Viscosity in water is of great importance to fish and other aquatic creatures. They need to move about in the water. To keep the water resistance down to a minimum, they have evolved special shapes. One thing that all these shapes have in common is that they are streamlined. Look at the apparently effortless way dolphins can swim alongside ships at sea. Incidentally, it is not just the body shape but also the nature of the outer skin that is important.

Air also has viscosity. Supersonic aircraft have to be specially designed to overcome so-called air resistance. Look at the sleek shape of these planes and compare them with the shape of fish. Concentrate on the *fuselage* of the plane and compare it to the *body* of the fish.

Sometimes we wish to increase the air resistance. A free-fall parachutist needs to increase air resistance dramatically to slow down before landing. The parachute opens up and causes a huge increase in this resistance. The landing without a parachute does not bear thinking about . . . ouch!

What two factors do you think affect the resistance of the air to motion?

One, using the parachute example, is the size of the object which is falling. If you can substantially increase the size of the falling object, you can correspondingly increase the resistive force. It is actually a bit more complicated than that. Think about the free-fall parachutist. If she dives in the fashion of a springboard diver, she falls with less air resistance than she would do with the familiar spread-eagle shape of the 'sky-diver'.

Another factor is the speed with which the object is moving. Generally speaking, the faster the object is moving, the greater is the air resistance. Our 'free-faller' will gradually pick up speed as she falls out of the aircraft. The air resistance gets greater and greater until eventually the upward drag of the air resistance exactly balances the downward force of gravity on the parachutist. The net force is now zero and the faller does not fall any faster. We say that she has reached **terminal velocity**.

By the way, this is an excellent example of the idea of balanced forces. There are two equal and opposite forces acting on the one body, the effects of which cancel. This is why the parachutist falls at a constant speed.

PRESSURE

Many people use the two words 'force' and 'pressure' interchangeably, as if they meant exactly the same thing. To a scientist, though, the two are very different.

We have looked at the concept of force in some detail. It is now time that we looked more carefully at the idea of pressure. In scientific terms, 'pressure' is defined as the 'force per unit area'. We need to think about just what this means.

Let's consider some examples. Think about going for a walk in some soft snow about half a metre deep. What would happen? You would sink right in. The downward force you exert on the top of the snow is too much for the soft stuff to support and down you go. What can be done about this? Well, you could try not going out in the snow. But if you live in an area where there is deep snow most of the winter, this suggestion is not much help. Fortunately, there is an alternative. If you could spread your weight out over a larger area of snow then it is possible that the snow could support you. This is the idea behind snow-shoes.

Have you ever been to one of those dance halls where they have beautiful polished wooden flooring? You know, the ones where they have signs up warning you that you are not allowed to wear stiletto heels. Have you ever wondered why? Is this not just prejudice against the fashion-conscious dancer? No, it certainly is not. When dancers wear flat shoes, their weight is spread out over a relatively large area. If you like, the wooden blocks share out the burden of holding up the dancer. Now think about how much less area there is under a stiletto heel. The force is much more concentrated. A tiny

piece of wooden floor has to support the same amount of weight as a much larger area did in the case of the flat shoes. In fact, stiletto heels can seriously mark a wooden floor.

At the local golf course, the ground becomes very soft when it has rained for only a few days. Whenever this happens there is a sign put up asking members to use only trolleys with wide wheels. Why is this? If a heavy bag of golf clubs is placed on a trolley with narrow wheels, the weight is concentrated over a smaller area than if wide wheels are used. Narrow-wheeled trolleys are much more likely to rut the soft ground than are wide-wheeled ones.

If you look at modern shoulder bags you will notice that they have narrow straps, but there are wider areas which can slide up and down so as to cover your shoulder. Why are they necessary? If you do not have this protection, the narrow straps can cut into your shoulder and be most uncomfortable. Imagine using straps made of thin cheese-wire . . .

In each of these examples, it is not just the force involved which has been important. The area over which the force acts has also been taken into consideration. The cheese-wire example shows what has to be done if the intention is to make the effect of the force more noticeable. In cases where the area over which the force acts is reduced, the pressure is increased. In cases where the area over which the force acts is increased, like the flat-soled shoes, the pressure is decreased.

You can now answer questions like 'Why are arrowheads pointed?', 'Why should knives be sharp?' and 'Why do workers working on top of weak roofs lay down planks to walk on?'

Pressure in gases

You do not talk about pressure just in terms of solid objects and the forces between them. When dealing with gases, one rarely talks about the force involved. Usually all that is considered is the pressure.

Weather forecasters often talk about areas of high and low pressure. What makes the air in the atmosphere have pressure in the first place? Just consider all the air sitting above you in the atmosphere. There is quite a lot of it, bearing down on you with the force of gravity. It is this that gives rise to pressure. The question is, with all that weight of air, why are we not just squashed flat on the ground?

The point about pressure in gases, and liquids for that matter, is that it acts *equally in all directions*. If that seems rather hard to swallow, just think what happens when you blow up a round balloon. It does not just expand opposite the inlet hole! No, it expands equally in all directions. Well, the air pressure all around us acts equally on *us* in all directions. If you jump up off the ground so that you are surrounded by air, you will find that the air pressure will act in all directions, up as well as down, forwards as well as backwards, left as well as right.

You might ask, 'Why don't we simply cave in, then?' The answer is that our bodies are also pressurized. The pressure inside our bodies pushes out with the same strength as the air pressure pushes in. We are in balance. In fact, astronauts have to wear pressure suits when in the vacuum of space because there is no air, and therefore no air pressure, in space. Without a pressure suit, the space traveller would simply explode as the pressure inside the body found no balancing pressure outside.

We measure air pressure with devices called **barometers**. A commonly found type is called an aneroid barometer. This uses a disc-shaped metal box the upper and lower surfaces of which are formed into concentric ridges to make it more flexible. If the pressure outside goes up, the box collapses until the pressure inside matches the pressure outside. If, on the other hand, the pressure outside drops, the box expands. A system of levers is attached to the centre of the box. The levers 'magnify' the motion so that a pointer can be seen to move, giving an indication of the air pressure.

What goes on inside the metal container of the aneroid barometer is of great interest to the study of gases. Assuming that the mass of gas is fixed – that is, that you end up with the same amount of gas as you started with – and that the temperature does not change, you find that if you increase the pressure of a gas, its volume decreases. Conversely, decreasing the pressure will cause the gas to expand and increase volume. This result is quite famous and is known as **Boyle's law**.

Pressure in liquids

The kind of pressure felt in liquids is much the same as in gases. In fact, the kind of pressure that acts equally in all directions is called **hydrostatic pressure**. Do you remember when you were a child you used to go paddling in ponds or rivers wearing your wellington boots? When you got in really deep, 10 cm or so, you probably felt your wellington pushing in on your feet. That is because the deeper you go under water, the higher the pressure gets. Water is, of course, much heavier than air. (Try comparing a bucket of air and a bucket of water, if you are doubtful!) This means that small increases in depth bring about larger increases in the weight of water above you that needs to be supported.

Divers have to watch the speed with which they change depth. Going down is not so bad, but they have to be very careful when coming back up, because the extra pressure of the water causes the pressure inside the body to increase. The body can withstand a certain amount of variation in this, but if you go too deep you will be crushed! The pressure of the blood is most important. The higher the pressure, the more easily gases such as the nitrogen and oxygen that we breathe can be dissolved in the blood. On the other hand, the lower the pressure, the less easy it is for the blood to dissolve these gases.

The effect of lowering the pressure in the blood too rapidly is a lot like opening the top of a lemonade bottle. While the lid is firmly attached, you may not even notice that there is carbon dioxide gas dissolved in the drink. Open the lid and *whoosh!* the drink fizzes away merrily. Well, the same sort of thing will happen to the blood of the diver if he or she is foolish enough to come up too quickly. We are exaggerating slightly, since the diver would have to depressurize extremely quickly for such frothing to occur. However, bubbles can form in the bloodstream. This is the cause of the dreaded **bends**.

Divers are also trained to breathe in and out as they swim upwards. Think what would happen if they did not. The pressure of the gas inside their lungs would drop as they went up because of the reduction in water pressure.

According to Boyle's law, this would cause the volume of the air in their lungs to increase. If they held their breath as they swam to the surface, they could damage their lungs.

SPRINGS AND THINGS

Although it does not seem to have much to do with springs at first, just think about modelling clay for a moment – or to be more precise, think about what happens to modelling clay when you apply a force to it. Yes, it will move faster and so on. Think a little harder and you will realize that, if you apply a pair of opposing forces to modelling clay (by pinching between finger and thumb, for example), it will squash up. We have just discovered another effect of forces.

☐   **Forces can make things change their shape.**

What happens to the modelling clay when you stop pinching it? The answer, of course, is that nothing happens. It remains squashed up. It has permanently changed shape. Another way of describing this is to say that the modelling clay has undergone a *permanent deformation*. Of course, modelling clay is not the only material that can be deformed in this way. Soft metals such as lead can also be easily deformed. Plumbers bend copper piping to take water round corners.

Now think about what would happen if you tried to pinch a block of rubber in the same way as the modelling clay. You can imagine that the rubber would change shape in a similar way to the modelling clay. It would probably be a bit more difficult to squeeze. You might have to pinch harder. The effect would be pretty much the same though. But what happens when you stop pinching? The rubber simply returns to its original shape. The deformation it suffered when you squeezed it was only temporary.

So far we have only considered deformations caused by squeezing. What happens if we try stretching? For the purposes of understanding this idea, think about a rubber band. If you hold the ends of a rubber band in your hands and pull, the band stretches. There is something else though. The band is able to pull back. The rubber band is said to be in a state of **tension**. If you pull harder, the rubber band will stretch more but it will pull back harder. You can carry on doing this until . . . ouch! The band breaks.

We can see, then, that there are two types of response to deforming forces. In the case of the modelling clay, the material simply changes shape and this shape is kept when the forces are removed. Such behaviour is called **plastic** (hence trade names such as 'Plasticine' are used to describe related products). On the other hand, the rubber block and rubber band pull back against the deforming forces, and when they are removed the rubber returns to its original shape. Such behaviour is called **elastic** (hence the name 'elastic bands').

Metal springs are specially made so that they behave in an elastic way. If you overstretch a spring, its behaviour stops being purely elastic and becomes partly plastic. It has been stretched so much that it has become permanently deformed.

A famous scientist called Robert Hooke discovered an interesting thing about springs. He discovered that, for the first part of the stretching, the amount of extension that is produced depends on the forces used to stretch it – in such a way that, if you double the force, you double the amount of stretch. Some springs are stiffer than others. For a stiff spring you get only a small increase in length or extension for the same force that will produce a larger extension in a weaker spring. To make it a fair test, of course, the springs have to start off the same length.

If you keep pulling harder and harder on a spring, eventually this relationship between extension and stretching force breaks down and the spring becomes more reluctant to extend. If you carry on pulling harder still, the spring becomes permanently deformed. That means that, even if you stop pulling altogether, the spring will not return to its original length. It is permanently stretched. You have exceeded the **elastic limit** and the spring behaves partially plastically. If you persevere and pull harder still, the spring finally gives up its resistance and begins to stretch and stretch until finally the **breaking point** is reached and the spring snaps.

You have probably noticed that springs are not only used to react to stretching forces. There are different springs for different purposes. You can also try to compress a spring. Many springs will push back at you if you try this. It is quite common that the amount of push needed to make a spring contract a certain amount matches the amount of pull needed to make it stretch by precisely the same amount.

Not only can you try to stretch things and push them together, but you can try to deform things in other ways. For example, you can try to twist a rubber band. If you have ever tried winding up rubber-band-driven toys, you will know that the band resists the twisting forces and untwists back.

For gases and liquids, it is not easy to think about forces pushing and pulling them. Instead it is more relevant to talk about changing the pressure on them. If you increase the pressure on a sample of gas that you have trapped, you will see that it will push back and will shrink its volume. Put your thumb over the end of a bicycle pump and push on the handle and you will get the idea. Gases can readily be compressed in this way. The same thing is definitely not true for liquids. It is often said that liquids are incompressible. This statement is not very far from the truth.

A large part of material science is devoted to the study of how materials react to being stretched, twisted, squeezed and pressurized. The subject can get very complex indeed. Perhaps you now have a better understanding of what you mean when you talk of a material being 'strong'.

FLOATING AND SINKING

Everyone knows that some things, like a beach-ball, float in water, whereas others, like a cannon-ball, sink.

Think carefully about what is needed for a beach-ball to float. The ball has mass and therefore is attracted to the Earth with the force of gravity. We call this the **weight**. Weight is a force which acts downwards. In order for a ball to float it has to remain stationary in the water – provided, that is, that the water itself is still. If it is acted upon by a force, Newton's first law tells us that a body will be caused to move from a state of rest. Since the floating ball does not move, we must deduce that there is no *net* force acting upon it. There must therefore be an upward force acting on the ball which is equal, but of course opposite, to the force of gravity.

Now, what about the cannon-ball that sinks in water? If it is released from rest as it is sitting in the water, it is caused to move downwards. Newton's law again tells us that there must therefore be a force acting downwards. This could be for one of two reasons. First there could be no force other than gravity acting on the cannon-ball. Second, it could be that the same upward force that causes the beach-ball to float acts on the cannon-ball, but it is not strong enough to cancel out its weight: after all, a cannon-ball would weigh more than a beach-ball of the same size. As we shall soon see, the latter is the case.

Have you ever noticed what happens to a floating object if it is held under the water and then released? Think about what happens to a beach-ball which is treated in this way. Of course, it rushes to the surface and even jumps out of the water. When a floating body is completely submerged in this way, there must be a net force acting upwards. This means that the upward force which causes it to float in the first place is now stronger than the force of gravity and the object moves up.

When an object, like the beach-ball, is floating in the water, you will notice that there is always a proportion of the ball *under* the water. If too much is under the water, it will pop up; if too little is below the surface, it will settle down. This gives us a clue about how floating and sinking works.

Think about the forces, resulting from water pressure, on a cube which is half submerged in water, as shown in this diagram.

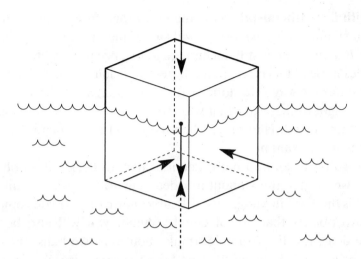

As we saw in the section on pressure, there will be water pressure acting on all faces of the cube which are underwater. The front face feels a force towards the back due to this pressure. Similarly, the back face of the cube feels a force towards the front. The two forces cancel each other out. The cube moves neither to the front nor to the back. In the same way, the forces on the sides of the cube cancel out.

What about the forces on the top and bottom faces? The bottom face feels the strongest force of all because it is the deepest face; and the deeper in the water you get, the higher the pressure becomes. The top face is above the surface of the water and therefore does not feel a force due to the water at all. The result is that the water pushes upwards on the cube. We call this upward force which the water exerts the **upthrust**.

If the cube is floating, it is because this upthrust is exactly balancing the weight. If a floating cube is pushed down and released, the increased pressure on the lower surface will cause the upthrust to increase above the level of the weight, and the cube will move upwards just like the completely submerged beach-ball. On the other hand, if the cube is not deep enough then the upthrust will not be able to support the weight, and the cube will sink until the weight is balanced. The deeper the cube sits, the greater is the upthrust.

If the cube is completely under the water, there will still be an upthrust because the bottom surface is lower than the top surface. This means that the pressure on the lower surface is greater than that on the upper surface, so the upward force on the lower surface is greater than the downward force on the upper surface. This results in an upthrust.

However, at a certain point, **pushing the cube lower in the water no longer causes an increase in the upthrust because, although the upward force is**

increased with increasing depth, so is the downward force. The upthrust has reached a maximum value. An object will sink if the upthrust produced when it is *completely submerged* is still not enough to balance its weight.

Archimedes noticed this effect in the times of ancient Greece. He looked at it a slightly different way. He noticed that the *strength* of the upthrust was equal to the weight of the water that was moved out of the way to make room for the object immersed. Naturally, when the object is completely immersed, the upthrust is at a maximum.

Before we go on to look in more detail at how to decide if an object will float or sink, we need to think about the idea of **density**. Basically, the density of a material is the mass in kilograms of 1 cubic metre of it. If you compare the masses of two objects that are of equal volume, you will also be able to compare the densities. For example, think about our two balls, the cannon-ball and the beach-ball. Imagine they are both the same size. Which will have the greater mass? Which has the greater density?

Now let us return to Archimedes. When the cannon-ball is immersed in the water, it displaces its own volume of water. The water is less dense than the cannon-ball, so the mass and therefore the weight of water displaced is less than the weight of the cannon-ball. The upthrust is therefore less than the weight of the ball, so it sinks. The beach-ball is much less dense than the water. It does not have to settle very far before the weight of the water that it has displaced is equal to the weight of the ball, so it floats.

> **In general, bodies which are less dense than water will float, whereas bodies which are more dense will sink.**

In this way, the idea of density is not only fundamental to the weight of objects (weight is one of the important factors at work with regard to floating and sinking), but it also tells us something else about floating and sinking. The density of the medium in which things can be immersed also has an effect.

So far we have thought only about water. But what about a substance that, for a given volume, weighs less than water – one that is less dense? Petrol is an example. Do you think it would provide the same amount of upthrust as water? Well, a piece of hardwood that only just floats in water would probably sink if immersed in petrol. Less dense liquids can provide less upthrust to counteract the weight of the immersed object. Petrol is a rather extreme example, so let's try something more realistic. Water can be 'fresh', from rivers or streams, or salty, as in seas and oceans. The more saline the water becomes, the higher the density. It follows that ships carrying goods round the world need to be conscious of the changes in density between river ports and those directly on the coast. A heavily laden ship loading in, say, the salty Caribbean, will settle progressively deeper in the water if it attempts to sail up the Amazon to unload at Manaus. It may not even arrive!

Hang on a minute though, what about the ships? They are made of steel but they float, don't they? Well, yes, they do. The thing here is that the metal is shaped so that it is hollow. This means that it is possible to displace enough water to produce an upthrust which will support the ship before the level reaches the deck. If, as may happen in a storm, the water slops over the top and fills the hull of the ship, it will surely sink.

> **The critical factors in floating and sinking are the weight and shape of the object as well as the density of the liquid in which it is immersed.**

Think about the class investigation which is carried out with small children and view it with new eyes. The child takes a piece of modelling clay. He or she drops it in a tank of water and sees it plummet to the bottom. The weight of the modelling clay is more than the upthrust provided by the water. Next the child changes the shape of the modelling clay. It is made thin, and the sides are bent up to make a shape like a pudding bowl. It is gently put in the water. Hey presto! What once sank now floats. The weight has not changed, but the shape has. The new shape is able to displace more water than the original, and as a result is able to get more upthrust than before.

TURN, TURN AGAIN

Turning forces

Have you ever noticed that, if you push a door near the handle, it is easier to open or close than if you push it near the hinge? If you have not, go away and try it right this minute! How can this be? Surely it must be the case that only *one* force is needed to operate the door. How can it matter whereabouts you apply the force?

Think about what happens to your hand when you push near the door-handle. Your hand moves through a large arc. If, on the other hand, you push near the hinge, your hand moves through only a small arc. If you like, your effort is more concentrated when you push near the hinge. You are in fact turning the door about a pivot at the hinge when opening and closing it.

When you are dealing with forces that cause turning effects, it is therefore not enough to talk simply about the size of the force; you need to know about the place where the force is applied. When dealing with turning forces, the distance from the point of rotation needs to be taken into account. The combination of the nearest distance from the pivot and the strength of the force is called the **moment of the force about the point.**

In practice, the size of the moment of the force increases with the strength of the force and also with the distance from the pivot. This effect can be seen in many everyday examples. Consider the problem of the fully grown person who wishes to entertain a youngster on a see-saw. If both people sit at the end of the see-saw, the adult will not balance with the youngster. If the adult moves towards the pivot, the moment of the force of their weight about the pivot (this really means the turning effect) is decreased. If he or she moves near enough to the pivot, the adult will balance with the youngster and the fun can begin.

The see-saw is an example of a device called a **lever**. What a lever does is enable the turning effect (moment) of a force of small strength to balance the turning effect of a larger force, simply by varying the relative distances from

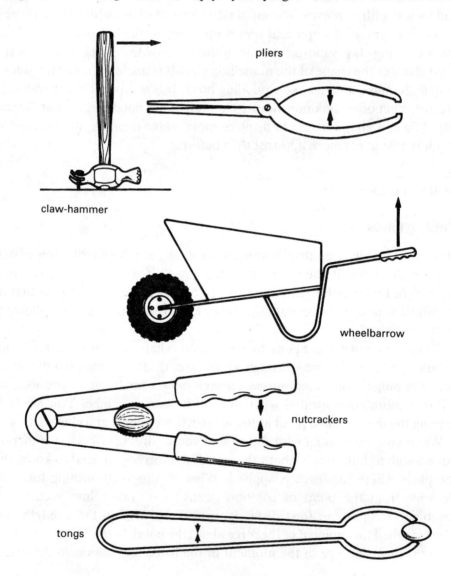

pliers

claw-hammer

wheelbarrow

nutcrackers

tongs

the pivot. A small force a long way from the pivot can easily balance a large force near the pivot. A few examples are illustrated on page 32.

Motion in a circle

Levers and similar devices turn through arcs but rarely move in complete circles. Let's look at motion in a circle. First of all, think about whirling an object round on a piece of string. Ask yourself the question, 'Have you ever seen a piece of string push?' The answer is obvious. Strings are very good at pulling forces, but they are no use for pushing.

Go back to our object on the end of the piece of string. If it is moving in a circle, it is clear that it is constantly moving, but equally that it is constantly changing direction. According to Newton's first law, a body will continue moving in a straight line unless acted upon by a force. The object must be acted upon by a force because it is not moving in a straight line. What is providing the force, and in which direction does the force act?

As we have said, strings are good at pulling. It is clear that the string is providing the force because if the string suddenly breaks the object will move off at a tangent. It will move in a straight line instead of a circular path. Since the string can only pull, the force on the object must be along the string towards the centre of the circle.

A common misconception

Many people get the wrong idea about this force. They are often heard to talk about forces acting to throw the object *outwards*. They call this **centrifugal force**. Centrifugal force exists only in the imagination. To explain this, think about going for a ride in the car. As the car turns a sharp left-hand corner, you, the passenger, feel as if you are being pushed to the right of the car. Why is this?

Unless acted upon by a force, you will continue to move in a straight line. In order that you turn the corner with the car, something must push you. You are in fact pushed to the *left*. What pushes you to the left? The answer is that the right-hand side of the car pushes you to the left. Your body wants to carry straight on, but the right side of the car cuts across your path and forces you to move to the left with it. This gives you the *impression* that you are being thrown to the right. If you were foolish enough to be leaning out of the right-hand window when the car turned the left-hand corner, the car would turn left but you would carry on moving in a straight line – straight through the window.

YELP!

SCREECH

LUCY MADDISON

Remember, when moving in a circle there is always a force acting. This force, called centripetal force, always acts towards the centre of the circle.

Let's think about another example of motion in a circle: a satellite in a circular orbit. What provides the force in this case? Why, gravity of course. Gravity always acts towards the centre of the Earth. Incidentally, you should now understand why it is that satellites do not need to have motors running all the time to keep moving. In space there is very little (practically no) air to cause air resistance. According to Newton's law, the satellite just keeps on moving.

The fact that the force of gravity, during circular orbit, always acts at right angles to the motion means that it causes the satellite to change direction, but does not cause it to slow down or speed up.

One of the unsurprising things about orbits is that, the higher the orbit, the longer it takes to complete one circuit. (Actually, the relationship is not as simple as direct proportionality, but the idea is good enough for our purposes.) If a satellite is placed in orbit above the Equator, it is quite possible for it to be positioned at such a height that it takes exactly 24 hours to complete one orbit. If it is moving in the same direction as the Earth's rotation, it orbits once every time the Earth turns. This means that it is always right above the same part of the Earth's surface. Such an orbit is called a **geo-stationary orbit**. It is very useful to have television transmitting satellites placed in geo-stationary orbit, so that we only have to point our aerial dishes to them and we are set up for good. If they were in some other orbit we would have to keep re-aligning our dishes to track the path of the satellites.

A FEW FINAL THOUGHTS . . .

Force is a fundamental aspect of the physical sciences. We experience the effects of force on a large scale at every moment of our lives. For example, the balancing of force is what gives our bodies a distinctly human form. The pressure of air pressing all around us is balanced by the hydrostatic pressure within our bodies. Very convenient!

Force plays a part in every observable event. It helps to explain how things start moving, stop or change direction. We can stand back and marvel at the sheer genius of a scientist like Newton who, many, many years before the advent of space travel, was able to predict accurately the movement of bodies in deep space. Similarly, Newton was able to see beyond the constraints of planet Earth and realize that *all* bodies exert gravitional force, and thus to formulate a law of universal gravitation.

Force is also central to events at a microscopic level. Later in this book we will look at issues that concern matter and electricity. We will see that force plays a fundamental part in the relationships that affect small particles.

Force is what makes things happen. When anything happens something called 'Energy' is transferred, and it is to energy that we next turn our attention.

Chapter 2

Energy

INTRODUCTION

The word 'energy' in our everyday speech has a wide variety of meanings. We say, for example, 'We have no energy.' What does this mean? Can we eat some food and *replace* some energy? Can we actually have *no* energy? We could also say that exercise is a way of using up energy. Is this so? Can we *use up* energy?

Contrast this with the idea of exercise being good for you because it *builds up* your energy! With machines we can say things like 'Machines require energy to work.' Energy here is perceived as being like a substance or fuel that is used up or replaced.

'Energy' is a word that we use all the time, but it means lots of different things to us!

TOWARDS A SCIENTIFIC VIEW OF ENERGY

As you can see, we are not very careful about how we use the word 'energy' in everyday speech. The meaning is different depending upon the context. This is not good enough for scientific use. The reason is that science is itself a context, and we need to define our terms carefully so that we all agree to interpret the word 'energy' in the same way. To do otherwise would lead to confusion.

What we will now try to do is begin to understand what a scientist means by the term 'energy', by looking at some examples of its use in a scientific sense. In this way it is hoped that more will be learned and *understood* than offering some remote formal definition.

To start with, let's look at the example of eating food. Why do we have to eat? There are a great many reasons for this, but one of them is that food supplies us with the energy that we need.

What do we need this energy for? As animals, we *move* around for lots of reasons. These include being able to find and then to prepare the food we eat. We also have movements within our bodies in order to keep us alive. We refer here to things such as breathing and heartbeats. Humans are warm-blooded animals. That means that we do not rely on atmospheric warmth for our bodies to function. We are able to produce our own heat energy from our food. You can see, of course, that energy is something that we need in order to live our everyday lives.

Let's look at what happens to this energy from start to finish. We might get our energy from our food, so there must be a store of energy inside the food itself. Our food is really a complex set of chemicals. We can say that the energy is stored in a chemical form.

In essence, we need energy from food to support a whole range of body processes that enable us to go out and seek more food and to reproduce our own kind! These body processes – digestion, respiration and so on – are really quite complex. During respiration energy is made available to the muscles to allow them to move. We could say that energy stored in a chemical way is released and is transferred to movement energy.

The next question is, where does the food get its energy from? The answer depends upon the food material that you ate. If it was meat, then the animal more often than not ate plant material as its source of food. If you ate vegetable matter, then the plant obtained its energy from the Sun.

A process called **photosynthesis** enables plants to produce sugars from sunlight, water and carbon dioxide. So the energy in sunlight is *transferred* into sugars and is stored there in a chemical form. Some plants may then convert these simple sugars into starches or even into oils. We eat the plant material and transfer this food energy into energy of movement as we use our muscles. Scientists call this energy of movement **kinetic energy**.

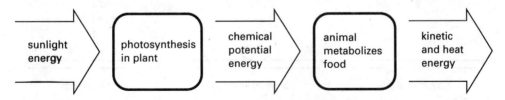

Let's try to stop thinking about food for a moment and consider another example. Imagine you are out near the seaside on top of a cliff. The ground is covered in grass and a game of rounders is going on. The ball has been well struck and . . . oh, no . . . it is rolling close to the edge of the cliff. It is not moving very fast as it reaches the edge and tumbles over. If we think about the energy of a slowly moving ball we would say that it has only a small amount of kinetic energy. As it falls from the top of the cliff, it picks up speed. We would say that its kinetic energy is increasing as it gets faster. Any object that falls from any height would find that its speed increased. Anything high has the potential to fall to a lower position and pick up speed as it does so. The ball at the top of the cliff therefore has a store of energy waiting to be transferred into kinetic energy as it falls. We call this stored energy **potential energy**. As the ball falls, this potential energy is gradually transferred into kinetic energy. Kinetic energy increases at the expense of the potential energy.

There is a concrete roadway at the bottom of the cliff. As the ball strikes the ground, it bounces back and is moving up the cliff again. When discussing kinetic energy it does not make any difference which way the ball is moving. As the ball goes up in the air, it is slowed down by gravity and the kinetic energy is transferred back into potential energy once again. However, the ball does not reach the top of the cliff; it stops short. At this highest point, all the kinetic energy has been transferred into potential energy and yet the ball has less potential energy than it had when it just rolled off the top of the cliff at the start.

To find out where this energy has gone, we need to look more closely at the bounce. The ball starts off moving downwards quite quickly. It has a lot of kinetic energy. As the ball strikes the ground it becomes distorted. This is shown in the sequence below.

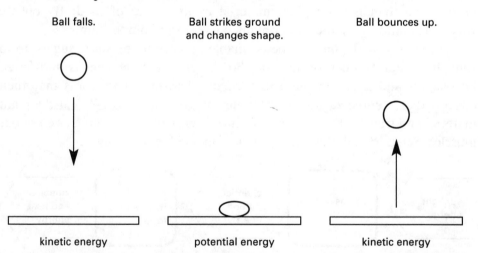

Ball falls.	Ball strikes ground and changes shape.	Ball bounces up.
kinetic energy	potential energy	kinetic energy

Quickly the ball is brought to rest. Where has the kinetic energy gone? The squashed ball has the potential to unsquash itself and fly upwards again, so there is **potential energy stored in the squashed ball**. This is transferred into kinetic energy again as the ball moves upwards. If you had been standing on the road when the ball hit the ground, you would certainly have heard the impact. Some of the energy has been transferred into sound energy. Also some of the energy will have been transferred into heat energy at the point of impact. If you take hold of the ball when it finally stops bouncing around, you will find that it feels warmer. This effect is particularly noticeable in the case of squash balls. Most players warm up before playing a game. As well as loosening up their muscles and improving their co-ordination, this has the effect of warming up the ball. The change of temperature of the ball affects how well it bounces.

Let's look at another example. This time think about a battery-driven torch, shining bright into a dark sky. A beam of light makes its way upwards, carrying light energy with it as it goes. What happens to this light energy? Some of it is absorbed by particles in the atmosphere and some of it is just scattered, but there may well be some that escapes the atmosphere and reaches space. Astronauts have reported being able to see the lights of major cities in the night. This light energy does not just disappear when it reaches space. It carries on travelling until it is absorbed by some particle. This may take millions of years. Light from distant galaxies has taken this long to reach us. You may think that the light energy gradually gets weaker as it gets further away. This would explain why distant stars which are often much brighter than our Sun appear so faint. Actually the reason is that the light spreads out into a cone as it travels through space, so although it looks fainter, it is really only more spread out.

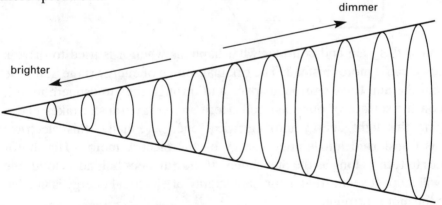

So where does the torch get its light energy from? Since it needs a battery to run, the answer must be that it gets its original supply of energy from the battery. The battery is made from a number of chemicals. This allows it to have a store of energy in a chemical form. A battery is able to transfer this energy into electrical energy. When a complete circuit is made, an electric current can flow. It is in the light bulb itself that this electrical energy is transferred into light energy and also some heat energy. If you touch a light bulb that has been glowing for some time, you will feel the heat. In fact, the filament is glowing white-hot. It is the transfer of electrical energy into light energy and heat energy which enables us to make use of the torch.

Think about a modern solar-powered calculator, converting light energy to electrical energy. This is another example where electrical energy is involved. This time there is no battery to provide the source of energy. Instead a solar cell is used. This is a device, based on silicon, which is able to convert sunlight directly into electrical energy. It is a very clever device indeed and not all that expensive. One of the most popular uses of this solar cell is to produce the electrical energy needed to run electronic calculators.

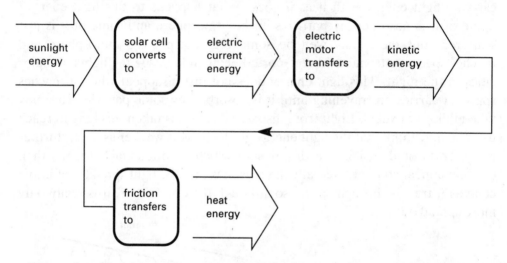

Now take this idea and consider what happens when it is used to drive a miniature electric motor instead. The original source of energy is the Sun. The light from the Sun travels through space and through the atmosphere until it arrives on the surface of our solar cell. Here an energy transfer takes place, converting this light energy into electrical energy. Finally, this electrical energy is transferred into kinetic energy by the electric motor. The motor continues to turn as long as the Sun shines. If the Sun goes behind a cloud, the motor will stop. It seems that a constant supply of electrical energy is needed to keep the motor turning.

This sounds wrong. Once the motor is turning, it has kinetic energy. What happens to this kinetic energy when the current stops supplying the motor with electrical energy? The motor grinds to a halt. In other words, the kinetic energy seems to be simply disappearing. If you feel the motor, it is likely to be warm. This is because there is always friction acting to oppose the motion. Friction converts the kinetic energy into heat energy, which is dissipated into the surrounding air. The constant supply of electrical energy is needed to make up for the steady drain of energy from the system as heat. If the motor were on completely frictionless bearings, the current would be needed to start the shaft turning, but when it reached the required speed the current could be switched off and the motor would continue to rotate.

Just one more example for the moment. A stone is hurled into the air and lands in a pond. As it leaves the hand, it has kinetic energy. This is steadily transferred into potential energy as it goes higher in the air. At the top of its flight all the energy is potential. This is then transferred into kinetic energy as the stone falls. When it strikes the water, the stone loses its kinetic energy but something happens to the water. Ripples or waves are formed. The water in the vicinity of the ripple moves up and down. There is kinetic energy of the water here. There is also potential energy because some of the water is raised up. Waves are means of transferring energy, usually in the form of potential and kinetic energy, from one place to another. As the ripple spreads out, it becomes less noticeable: the energy is gradually dissipated over an ever-increasing wavefront.

So what can we learn from these examples?

To make sense of the examples we have considered, we have to try to answer some basic questions. First of all, we have to decide whether or not any energy was involved in the process. In every example this was obviously the case. There is nothing special about the examples chosen. It is possible to generalize from them to conclude that **whenever anything happens energy is involved**. How is the energy involved when something happens? The crucial thing here is that the energy is *transferred*. In order for anything to happen, energy must be transferred. It is the transfer that is of paramount importance.

This takes us a step nearer to understanding just what 'energy' is. It is something that is transferred whenever something happens. The next questions to be addressed centre around where the energy comes from, and where it finally goes to. Is it possible to 'make' energy from nothing? As far as we know, the answer to this question is *no*.

But it is never possible to be sure about such things. Scientific theories are made up to try to make sense of the universe. We test those theories to try to find flaws in them. The harder we try to disprove theories and fail, the more confident we are that the theory is valid. There is no such thing as a proved theory. So all that can be said is that we believe that **energy can be neither created nor destroyed**.

Having made the point that this is only a theory, we should point out that it is at the core of our beliefs about the way of the universe and that, in all of the countless number of experiments and observations that have been made, it has never been seen to have been contradicted – and this includes what we know about distant galaxies. It would be devastatingly surprising if it were ever proved to be false. This is the well-known statement of the **conservation of energy principle**. Here we are talking about the fact that the amount of energy that we have at the start of a process is the same as the amount that we have at the end.

Try not to confuse this idea with energy conservation in the sense of trying to stop heat escaping from a heated building, for example. This is an example of how using a term like 'conservation' in relation to 'energy' in ordinary speech can be ambiguous.

The principle of the conservation of energy has some important consequences for us. It means that we have to do the job of accountants, as it were, and balance the books. We have to measure the energy that goes into a process and trace it to see where it all goes. Energy is supplied in one form, in the process it is transferred into another form, and it can all be traced. In this way, the process is a linear one and not cyclic. This means that, unlike many natural processes (the water cycle, for example), there is no such thing as an energy cycle. It has a linear progression.

Let's try to trace the source of the energy in all of the examples we have thought about so far. As we saw in the food example, the original source of energy is the Sun.

If we ask how the ball got to the top of the cliff, the answer will probably be that someone carried it up there. Where did the person get the energy from? They got it from the food they ate, which allows us to trace the source of energy back to the Sun.

The chemicals in the torch were produced in a chemical factory. Zinc metal, which forms one of the important chemicals in a typical zinc–carbon battery, has to be extracted from its ore. The supply of energy needed to extract and refine this metal can be traced back to the Sun through fossil fuels. We will look at them in more detail later on.

Obviously the source of energy for the solar cell was the Sun.

A person threw the stone into the pond. Once again this energy comes from the Sun in the first place, just like the energy needed to carry the ball up the cliff.

The original source of energy is nearly always the Sun. But there are some examples where this is *not* the case. Tidal energy, geothermal energy and nuclear energy are cases in point. With nuclear energy it is the disintegration of materials like uranium that releases energy. These materials were made up inside stars which were burning brightly long before our own Sun, so although the energy cannot be traced back to our Sun, the energy does originate from *a* sun. For more detail about this, see the section on nuclear energy on pages 57–8.

Where does all the energy go? This is a good question. The energy involved in our examples can never be used up, yet we seem unable to make further use of it! This is why we need a constantly replenished supply from the Sun. The energy which we transfer in order to make things happen becomes steadily more and more spread out. We could say it becomes **dissipated**. One of the most important ways in which this happens is when it is transferred into heat energy.

This transfer happens in a number of ways. For example, friction is a force which opposes motion. Whenever motion occurs, friction is constantly transferring kinetic energy into heat energy. When the Sun's rays strike the Earth, one of the largest effects they have is to cause heating. Heat is an important way that we can observe energy, and as such it needs to be studied in more detail.

In what other ways can we recognize energy? Heat energy, kinetic energy and potential energy have already been mentioned. Other important ways that energy appears include chemical energy, light radiation energy, electric current energy and sound or wave energy. There is also energy associated with constant electric and magnetic fields. Energy can be found in a huge number of different disguises. It is important to realize that it is not the *form* which the energy takes that is so important, but rather the *transfer* between forms that takes place. It is when such a transfer takes place that something happens.

HEAT ENERGY

According to the conservation of energy principle, energy can neither be created nor destroyed. The energy we use normally ends up as heat. The question arises, why cannot we simply recycle the used energy by making use of the heat energy? To answer this vitally important question, we need to discuss heat energy in much more detail.

Another word that we often meet when discussing heat is 'temperature'. Many people use the two words interchangeably as if they are the same thing. We have already decided that heat is one way that we can recognize the presence of energy, but what about temperature?

People often say that temperature is a measure of the hotness or coldness of a body. Care is needed when using subjective terms like hot or cold. Presumably what is meant by this is how hot or cold something *feels*.

Feel, however, is a very unreliable way of determining temperature. An activity often tried in primary schools is to place three washing-up bowls on a table and to fill one with ice-cold water, one with quite hot water (as hot as the children can stand safely) and the third bowl with tepid water. If children are asked to place one hand in the hot and the other hand in the cold bowl for a few minutes, they find that when they try to decide whether or not the middle bowl is warm or cool, their two hands give conflicting information. We need to be more careful when deciding what is meant by temperature, and not to rely on feel alone.

Let's step back from trying to define temperature and think instead of what we mean when we say that one body is at a higher temperature than another. Take a hot cup of tea placed outside on a cold day, for example. How can we claim that the tea is at a higher temperature than the surrounding air? We could try using a thermometer. What is a thermometer but a device for measuring temperature? If we define temperature using a thermometer as a basis, we are saying that it is 'something measured by thermometers' and we have gone round in a circle!

Instead, let's think about this cup of tea. After a short while the tea will have 'gone cold', as we say. What we are really saying is that the tea has lost heat to the surrounding air. In fact, whenever two objects are placed in such a way that heat can be transferred from one to the other, we find that heat will flow until such time as a state of equilibrium has been reached. When this state has been reached, we say that the two bodies are at the same temperature. The body that was originally at the higher temperature has lost heat, and the body that was at the lower temperature has gained heat.

> **Heat always travels from a body at a high temperature to a body at a lower temperature.**

We now know what we mean when we say that one body is hotter than another. But we still have not defined what temperature is! In order to do this you need to know more about the structure of matter itself, and this is covered in Chapter 3.

It is worth breaking off our discussion of heat and temperature here to consider how heat energy is transported around. First of all, every body that contains heat energy is constantly emitting heat in the form of **radiation**. (Radiant heat is called infra-red radiation, by the way.) If you place your hand in front of a red-hot object, like the bars of an electric heater, you will feel this radiant heat. This is the way that the heat from the Sun is transported to the Earth. Just feel the warm sunshine the next time you get the chance. The hotter the body, the greater is the rate at which it is emitting this radiation. This means that a hotter body will radiate more heat to a cooler body than the cooler body will radiate to the hotter one. This results in a net gain of heat energy by the cooler body and a net loss of heat energy by the hotter one.

A second method by which heat energy is transported is **conduction**. Here heat flows through the material of the body itself. If you place a metal spoon in a saucepan of boiling water, you will soon find that the handle becomes too

hot to hold. This is because heat has been conducted through the metal of the spoon. Some materials, like metals, conduct heat better than others. Heat is always conducted from a hot part to a cold part.

Finally, heat energy stored in a fluid can flow as the fluid itself flows. Of course, this only happens in liquid and gases. Hot air rises, and as it does so it carries the heat energy with it. This method of heat transport is called **convection**.

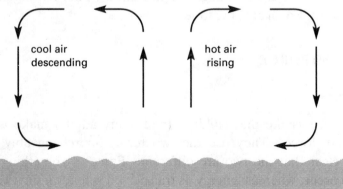

Heat energy and temperature are not the same thing. Think about this. You take an empty kettle to the seaside and fill it up with sea water. Ask yourself which is at the higher temperature, the water in the kettle or the water in the sea. The answer is obvious, isn't it? They are both the same. Now ask yourself which has more heat energy in it. This time you have to think a bit before you decide that the sea has more heat energy in it because there is a lot more of it.

Suppose that we now put some extra heat into the kettle so that it comes to the boil. It still does not have as much heat energy as the entire ocean does it? Now we come to the crux of the matter. Although there is less heat in the kettle, the heat it does contain is much more useful than all the lower-temperature heat energy in the sea. For a start, it is much easier to get the heat out and transfer it to get something to happen. The higher the temperature associated with the heat, the more useful it is. The lower the temperature, the more spread out or dissipated the heat energy becomes. High-temperature heat can be made to run turbines to generate electricity or to produce motion in motor vehicles. Lower-temperature heat that is formed as a by-product of such processes is much less useful. In fact, power stations have large cooling towers to remove the 'useless' low-temperature heat energy.

When we talk of using up our supply of energy, we do not mean that it exists, is consumed and then no longer exists. Remember the conservation of energy principle. Energy cannot be created or destroyed. What we do is take energy in a useful form, use it to make something happen and in so doing transfer the energy into a less useful form. **We use up the usefulness and not the energy itself**.

What happens to all this heat that is constantly being generated? Surely the Earth will just keep on getting hotter. The answer is that just as the Sun is constantly radiating energy into space, some of which the Earth absorbs and we use, so the Earth is radiating heat energy into cold space. The Earth does not shine brightly as the Sun does because it is at a much lower temperature. But as any astronaut will tell you, the daylight side of the Earth can clearly be seen from space due to the reflected light from the Sun. By this same process, of course, we on Earth are able to see the Moon.

ENERGY AND FORCE

Kinetic energy

One common mistake that children (and many adults) make is to confuse 'energy' and 'force'. They use the two terms interchangeably. By now it should be clear that the two are different. 'Force' is something that causes changes to occur, whereas 'energy' is transferred whenever anything happens.

We can clarify this even further by considering the two terms together in relation to some examples.

Let's return to the possible effects of a force. A force can:

1. Cause a stationary object to start moving.
2. Cause a slowly moving object to move more quickly.
3. Cause a quickly moving object to move more slowly.
4. Cause a moving object to stop.
5. Cause a moving object to change direction.

A force can also:

6. Change the shape of an object.

The first five of these effects of a force are all linked to motion. The force causes the object to **change the way it moves**. To get a better understanding of what is going on, let's stop talking about general objects and return to our old friend, the supermarket trolley.

Since we are discussing motion and 'force', let's see how they relate to 'energy' and motion. One way of being sure that an object has some energy is to observe that it is in motion. Remember that the energy associated with motion is called **kinetic energy**. How do changes in motion affect the kinetic energy that a body possesses? Naturally enough, the faster a body moves, the more kinetic energy it will have.

(Actually things are not quite that simple. It is true that the faster the trolley moves, the more kinetic energy it has, but the relationship is not one of simple proportionality. If you double the speed, you do not double the kinetic energy. Rather you would quadruple the kinetic energy by doubling the speed unless you approach the speed of light. The reason for this is rather mathematical.)

Look at the first of the effects of a force. Our stationary supermarket trolley has been acted upon by a force. You pushed it! Consider the following questions:

What happened when you pushed the stationary trolley?

It started to move.

Now think about the energy. What happened to the kinetic energy of the trolley? Did it have any to start with?

No, it was stationary and stationary trolleys have no kinetic energy. They are simply not moving.

Did it have any kinetic energy after you pushed it?

Yes, you can tell because it was then moving.

Let's think about this more carefully. To begin with, the stationary trolley had no kinetic energy. *Then* you exerted a force on it by pushing. You caused it to move and it then had some kinetic energy. The force has caused the kinetic energy of the trolley to increase from zero. So some energy was transferred to the trolley when the force acted.

You can argue along similar lines when you think about the second effect a force can have. If you push a moving trolley to make it go faster, it gains more kinetic energy. There has been another energy transfer as the force acts.

Now what about when you heaved on the handle of the moving trolley and caused it to come to a grinding halt. Let's think about what has happened here.

What happened when you pulled the handle of the moving trolley?

It stopped moving.

Now think about the energy. What happened to the kinetic energy of the trolley? Did it have any to start with?

Yes it did. This must be true because the trolley was moving and moving objects have kinetic energy.

Did it have any kinetic energy after you pulled at it?

No, because it was no longer moving.

Think about this more carefully. The trolley started with some kinetic energy and then you exerted a force on it by pulling. This caused it to stop and it then had no kinetic energy. The force has removed the kinetic energy from the trolley. Energy was transferred from the trolley when the force acted.

The fourth effect a force can have has a similar result with respect to energy transfer. When you pull on the handle of your trolley to cause it to slow down, you *transfer kinetic energy* away from it.

So it seems that it is possible to *change the kinetic energy* possessed by the trolley *by pushing or pulling it*. This change can be an increase in kinetic energy if the trolley is made to start moving or to go faster. It may be that the kinetic energy is reduced or removed altogether if it is slowed down or stopped. You might be led to believe that the effect of a force is *always* to change the kinetic energy of a body.

To test out this hypothesis (scientists call a guess based on observations like this a **hypothesis**), you may care to consider the fifth effect a force can have. That is to say, it can cause a moving object to change direction. Now it is quite possible to change direction without changing speed. If the speed is neither increased nor decreased, there is no change in kinetic energy. This means that the hypothesis is either wrong or in need of refinement.

In the first four effects, the direction of motion and the direction of the force were the same (or opposite). They acted along the same line.

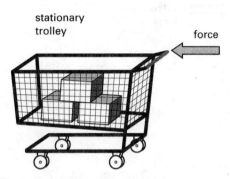

Stationary trolley starts to move.
Kinetic energy increases.

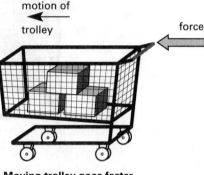

Moving trolley goes faster.
Kinetic energy increases.

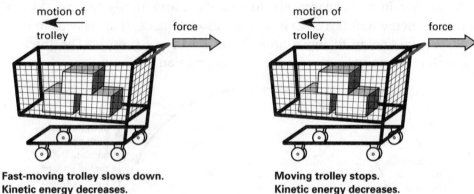

Fast-moving trolley slows down.
Kinetic energy decreases.

Moving trolley stops.
Kinetic energy decreases.

When all you want to do is make the trolley change direction, you need to apply a sideways force. The force is at right angles to the direction of motion. This only causes the trolley to change direction, it does not cause it to change speed, so there is no change in kinetic energy. (See the first illustration on page 50.) This is an important exception to our hypothesis.

We can now modify our hypothesis. We can say that **whenever a force acts on a moving body other than at right angles, kinetic energy is transferred to or from the body.**

This hypothesis is better. Energy is transferred when the point where a force acts is caused to move *so long as the movement is not at right angles to the line of action of the force.* This is given a special name by scientists. It is called **work**.

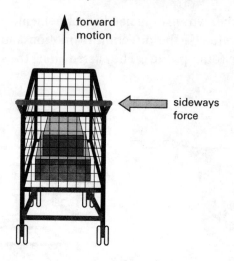

Conversely, *no energy* is transferred if the point at which a force acts does not move, or if it acts on a body at right angles to its motion.

A satellite in a circular orbit around the Earth needs to have lots of potential energy transferred to it to reach its high place. It also needs to have some kinetic energy to move around the Earth every orbit. The force of gravity on the satellite is at *right angles* to this motion.

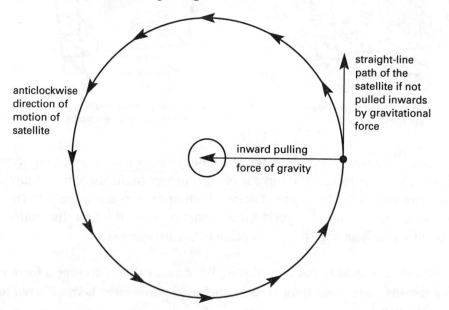

As a result, the force of gravity causes the satellite to *change direction* as it makes its way round the Earth, but it *does not cause a transfer of its kinetic energy*.

This is very important because it means that a satellite does not need a constant supply of fuel for energy just to keep it in orbit. Left to itself it would just go round and round for ever, like the Moon does. (Again life is not quite that simple in reality because artificial satellites do collide with tiny particles in space and this does slow them down very, very slightly so that eventually their orbits decay. However, this takes a long time and as such the satellite is not really being left to itself. The same thing happens to the Moon, but because it is so big the effect is not noticeable!) This whole idea is really fundamental to a knowledge of physical science.

☐   **When a force causes a change of motion in the ways described, energy is transferred.**

As far as the trolley was concerned, the energy involved was kinetic energy. The key question that now needs to be answered is, where does the energy come from and go to? The answer is . . . you!

Yes, that is right. You ate some food and that supplied your body with energy in a chemical way. You can now transfer that energy as you choose. One of the ways you can do this is by pushing a supermarket trolley and transferring energy to it as kinetic energy.

Unfortunately, when you slow the trolley down, you do not get the energy back in the same sort of way. If the trolley moved on to a slippery floor (where someone had just spilled a bottle of olive oil perhaps!) and you pulled on the trolley, you would find that it dragged you along. It would transfer kinetic energy to you. You cannot, however, get the energy transferred back into your muscles. To replenish this supply, you need food. You have transferred the energy from your muscles and it has become degraded. You have used up some of the usefulness. As you slow the trolley down to a stop, you transfer the kinetic energy is possessed into heat. The friction between your feet and the floor sees to this.

There are times when a force does work and yet does not transfer energy into a kinetic form. One example is where a force needs to be applied to counteract friction **to keep a moving object travelling at a constant speed**. The fact that the speed is constant means that there is no change in the kinetic energy of the object. You need constantly to push your supermarket trolley in order to keep it moving. You need to push against friction. Does this lack of transfer of energy to kinetic energy mean that no work is done? No, because if a force moves in the direction in which it acts, work *must be* done.

What happens is that the energy that you put in when you push the trolley is converted into heat energy at the points where friction acts. You put in work and friction transfers this into heat. Without your contribution, friction would simply convert the kinetic energy of the moving trolley into heat and the trolley would lose kinetic energy and slow down.

Potential energy

If you move with a force (that is, if you let the force push you), the force is said to do work on you. If you move faster because of this force, your kinetic energy increases as the force works on you. If, on the other hand, you move against the direction in which a force acts, you are doing work against the force, often at the expense of your kinetic energy.

The question arises, where does this energy go to? Sometimes, like when you apply the brakes to slow your car down, the work is done against friction (friction always opposes motion). This means that your kinetic energy is transferred to heat energy.

Here is another example to consider. A girl is playing ball in the playground. She hurls the ball into the air as high as she can. Think about what is happening to the energy of the ball. There is a force acting – the force of gravity. Gravity always acts downwards, of course. The ball is moving upwards against the direction of gravity.

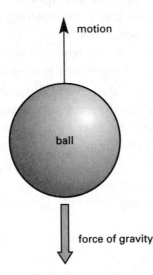

As the ball goes up, work is done against the force of gravity. This work is at the expense of the ball's kinetic energy and it slows down. Once again the question arises, where does this kinetic energy go to? The ball is moving upwards as it slows down.

If you let go of a ball from a great height, like the ball at the top of the cliff earlier in this chapter, it will fall and gain kinetic energy. We say that before it fell the ball had some stored or potential energy because it had the potential to fall. As it falls, the ball transfers potential energy into kinetic energy. On the other hand, the ball in our present case is moving upwards and its kinetic energy is being transferred. It is being transferred into potential energy.

Sometimes when you do work on a force, you do not dissipate your energy. Instead it becomes stored as potential energy which you can retrieve at a later date. Gravity is a force that allows you to store energy in this way. Such potential energy is, naturally enough, called **gravitational potential energy**.

There are other factors besides gravity that allow this sort of situation to occur. Another very important force is connected with magnetism.

All magnets have two poles. These are called north and south. The force rule for magnets is that **like poles repel one another and unlike poles attract**. This means that, if you hold two magnets with their north poles facing one another as shown in the diagram, there will be a force pushing the two magnets apart.

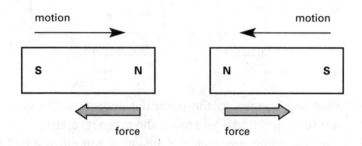

If you push the two closer together, you are moving the magnets against the force. This means that you are doing the work. Energy is transferred from you. Where does this energy go to?

To find the answer to this, think what would happen if you let the magnets go. The force that acts between them would push them so that they moved apart. This means that some kinetic energy would be transferred to them.

This is the same energy that was transferred from you to do the work against the magnetic force.

The energy has been stored as magnetic energy. When you pushed the two magnets closer together, you did work which transferred energy to them in the form of this potential energy. This is quite different from the previous gravitational case. The force of gravity is always attractive. The magnetic force we have just considered was repulsive.

If you pull apart two objects which are attracted to one another by a force like gravity, you will transfer potential energy into the system. If you allow the force to do the work instead, the potential energy is reduced as the objects move together.

The situation is reversed from repulsive forces. If you push together two objects which repel one another, you will transfer potential energy into the system. If you allow the force to do the work by pushing the two objects apart, potential energy is transferred to kinetic energy as the objects move apart.

You can simplify the situation by saying that in the magnetic and gravitational case, if you allow the force to do the work, potential energy is transferred out of the system into some other form, usually but by no means exclusively into kinetic energy. But if you do the work against the force, you transfer energy into the system as potential energy.

Here is another example. This time the magnets are placed with opposite poles facing. This, of course, means they will now attract each other.

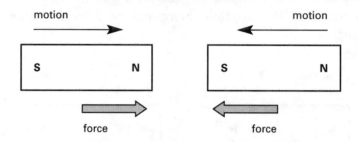

Ask yourself what will happen to the potential energy of the system if you move the magnets together, and if you move the magnets apart.

If you allow them to come together, it is just as if you allow a ball to fall to Earth, to which it is attracted by gravity. This means that the potential energy is transferred to kinetic energy as the magnets move together.

If you pull them apart, you are doing work which is transferred to potential energy. This is just like what happens when you raise a ball against the force of gravity by throwing it upwards.

This concept of forces like gravity and magnetism allowing potential energy to be built up is a most important one. It is central to the study of electricity. Here an electrical force acts in much the same way as the magnetic force (in fact, the two are related in a way that we will not go into, but scientists usually refer to the 'electromagnetic force'). This will be considered in more detail in Chapter 4.

Do not be misled into thinking that only these types of force can be linked to potential energy. Elastic forces like those in stretched or compressed springs can also store potential energy. To understand this just think what happens in the case of the catapult. You put a stone in the holder and pull the elastic as far as you can. You have done work against the elastic forces in the rubber bands. This transfers energy from you into elastic potential energy.

You can tell that this is so by observing what happens when you let go. The stone is acted upon by a force from the rubber bands. The force does the work and the potential energy in the bands is transferred into the kinetic energy of the stone as it flies through the air.

As you can see, there is a strong link between force and energy. The effect of an unbalanced force is to cause change as we described in Chapter 1. The main property of energy is that whenever anything happens energy is transferred. Change is something happening. Put the two together and you find that force causes change which means that energy is transferred.

FOSSIL FUELS

In terms of use of energy resources we live in peculiar times. One of the reasons for this is that for millenniums the main fuel burned by people to transfer energy was wood. The use of this natural raw material to satisfy our energy needs led to large-scale deforestation of the developed world. Industrial development was therefore strictly limited. The energy stored in the wood of the trees came directly from the Sun through the process of photosynthesis in the leaves. The rate at which energy could be transferred was limited to the rate at which the trees could convert solar energy.

Several hundred million years ago, ancient plants were storing energy transferred from sunlight in the same way as our modern plants do. Since then this ancient sunlight energy has been stored underground waiting for us to exploit it today. Such stores of energy are called **fossil fuels**. The limitation on the supply of usable fossil fuels means that their exploitation cannot go on indefinitely; there will soon come a time when they literally run out. But for a period of 300 years or so in the case of oil, mankind will have been able to exploit such fossil fuels and see the standard of living rise astronomically. We are living at a time when the exploitation of fossil fuels is at its peak. Compared with the half million or so years that we have been on the Earth, and hopefully the long future we have ahead of us, 300 years is but an instant!

Coal

Most of today's coal was formed from dense vegetation which grew around 300 million years ago during the so-called Carboniferous period. The climatic conditions of the areas in which coal-bearing rocks were to be laid down were rather different from today. It is thought that the vegetation was growing in swampy conditions such as river estuaries. The almost oxygen-less conditions of the decomposition process in the dark waters led to the production of organic material much like peat.

Coal was formed from the organic deposits when they were overlain by later water-borne sediments and 'sealed in' from later periods of erosion. The process was repeated many times, and for this reason coal deposits form strata or seams below the surface. Crustal movements led to deeper burial, and the high pressures and temperatures involved transformed the organic deposits into coal, and the muds and sand into sedimentary rocks. It is not certain whether any similar processes are working today to produce coal for the future, but it is evident that, even if they are, the rate at which coal is being produced is far exceeded by the rate at which it is being mined.

It is extremely difficult to estimate how long the coal reserves still available are likely to last. There are many factors involved, including the quantity of coal still unmined, the definition of what is mineable, the rate at which it is used and a great many imponderables. Having said all this, it is projected that production of energy from coal will peak in the next century and decline steadily as the millennium progresses. It is hoped that alternative sources of supply will be found before then.

Coal is mined by a variety of processes. The most expensive is via underground workings, where shafts and horizontal galleries give access to seams of coal. Open-cast mining for coal seams just below the surface of the ground is far cheaper, but may leave open scars on the landscape.

We have been talking about coal as if it were a single substance, but there are in fact many types. In increasing order of carbon content these are lignite, bituminous coal and anthracite. Bituminous coal is usually divided up into three grades or ranks. There is up to twice as much stored energy per tonne in anthracite as there is in lignite.

At present, by far the largest customer of the coal producers is the electricity generating industry. The production of coal gas from coal is currently more expensive than the use of natural gas, so natural gas is used. It is predicted that, as natural gas deposits run out, coal gas will once again become important.

Oil

Oil is a fossil fuel like coal, but it was formed in a very different way. It comes from the remains of sea creatures, like green plankton, which lived millions of years ago and whose remains decomposed on the seabed. This led to the dispersal of fine droplets of oil absorbed into these sedimentary rocks. Subterranean fluids like water and oil are constantly moving around. A mixture of water and oil will, of course, separate with the oil floating to the top. It should not be thought that there exist vast underground caverns with lakes of water and oil. Rather there are porous rocks into which the oil and water seep. Sometimes the oil seeps to the surface.

Oil stocks are conserved underground when they are trapped in various ways. This can happen where a layer of oil-bearing rock is covered with an impervious layer. Crustal movements can buckle or bend the layers of rock to produce a whole range of traps. By drilling through the capping layer, the oil can be allowed to rise to the surface. This may happen by naturally occurring pressure within the deposit, or by pumping. Oil deposits are usually much deeper than coal.

Once again, it is difficult to estimate exactly how long oil reserves are likely to last. The extremely high cost of exploration for oil means that the oil companies are reluctant to search too seriously for oil deposits without the prospect of short-term economic viability (around 20 years or so). It is expected that oil will become insignificant as an energy source in the next 100 years.

Oil can be processed by a method called **fractional distillation**. This separates the crude oil into its separate constituents. Each constituent provides us with a source of transferable energy. The uses range from aviation fuel and motor vehicle fuel, on the other hand, to fuel for large-scale furnaces used, for example, in the electricity generation industry.

Natural gas

Natural gas (as opposed to gas derived from the processing of coal or oil) is usually found in association with oil deposits. Typically, it is a clean-burning fuel without the problems of poisonous combustion products associated with coal or oil.

It is simple to transport by pipeline and the underground reserves themselves often form a huge natural storage structure. Nevertheless, transport from place to place may be required, in which case ships, lorries and trains can carry the gas under pressure in a liquefied form.

NUCLEAR ENERGY

Nuclear energy may be harnessed peacefully for the production of electricity. It is also central to the production of terrible weapons of mass destruction, with a growing number of countries holding stocks of nuclear missiles and other devices. In both power station and weapons applications, nuclear energy provides the same feature, heat energy.

With weapons there is a rapid and great release of intense heat energy – you will probably have seen pictures of atomic tests with a characteristic 'mushroom' of convected air (and lots of dust). In power stations, the heat energy from nuclear sources is very carefully controlled. Essentially, the heat energy from nuclear reactions replaces the heat energy from coal, gas or oil in a 'conventional' power station. Heat is used to turn water to steam and then to turn large fans called turbines. These are attached to generators which produce electricity.

So where does nuclear energy come from? There are two most useful ways that energy can be produced from nuclear reactions. These are called **nuclear fission** (splitting) and **nuclear fusion** (combining). Currently, all UK nuclear power stations use nuclear fission reactors. Only special materials are useful for nuclear fission. These nuclear materials include the substance uranium, which occurs naturally in Africa and Australia.

Uranium is first processed to make it into a more useful source of nuclear energy. The fissionable product, a special form of uranium called U235, is split in a specially controlled environment, the reactor core, and releases heat energy. The heat energy is removed from the core and then used to heat up the water to produce steam for the turbines.

There are many types of reactor design. The main differences between them are related to the means by which the heat energy generated during the fission process is removed from the reactor core and is passed to the generators to produce electricity. We can think of this agent of the removal of heat energy as a coolant, since it does not allow the reactor core to become too hot (and melt!) and in so doing transfers heat energy from the highly dangerous reactor core to enable the generation of steam to drive the turbines.

Some reactors use gas as a coolant. The **magnox reactor** has a core, surrounded by a steel pressure vessel, made of graphite blocks into which holes have been drilled. Into some of these holes **control rods** and **shut-down rods** are inserted. These allow the operators to change the output of the reactor. Into other holes the fuel elements are placed. The fuel elements are encased in a magnesium alloy which separates the radioactive fuel and waste products from the coolant. This type of reactor uses high-pressure carbon dioxide gas as the coolant. This is pumped through holes in the reactor core. From here it is allowed to leave the pressure vessel and pass through a heat exchanger, where it loses some of its heat to a supply of water, converting it into steam which is used to drive the turbines.

A newer type of gas-cooled reactor is the **advanced gas-cooled reactor (AGR)**. This is more efficient than the magnox reactor, chiefly because it runs at a higher temperature. This means that the fuel rods have to be encased in steel instead of magnesium alloy. These reactors also have carbon dioxide as the coolant. The heat exchanger is built inside the pressure vessel.

Some reactors like the **pressurized water reactor (PWR)** and the **boiling water reactor (BWR)** use water as a coolant. The fuel in such reactors needs to be more enriched with U235 than in the case of the gas-cooled reactors.

Nuclear waste

The problem of nuclear waste is one which must be taken very seriously if we are to embark on even larger-scale nuclear energy programmes. The supporters of nuclear energy constantly claim that the fear of such reactors in the minds of the public is based on ignorance. Chapter 3 includes more detail about the process involved. When you have read it you should be in a better position to judge for yourself.

RENEWABLE RESOURCES

So far we have discussed fossil fuels and nuclear energy. It was clear that fossil fuels will not be able to supply our energy needs for the long term. They will inevitably run out before too long. Similarly the raw material for nuclear fission reactors will not be available for ever. What we are dealing with here are finite resources with the end in sight.

When we talk of renewable resources what we really mean is resources which will last long into the future, so that humanity need not concern itself about them running out. New experimental nuclear *fusion* reactors rely on hydrogen, in a number of its different forms, as fuel. There is so much hydrogen available in the water of the seas that we need not worry about using up the Earth's supply. There are many more sources of energy that come into this renewable category. Many of them rely on energy which comes to us from the Sun, so it is fitting that we begin our section on renewable resources with solar energy.

Solar energy

The Sun is actually a giant nuclear fusion reactor in the sky. It will not be able to 'burn' for ever because it too will use up its supply of nuclear fuel and be destroyed. But this is not expected to happen for the next few thousand million years or so. To all intents and purposes solar energy is renewable.

The Sun radiates its energy into space. A tiny proportion of this total output falls upon the Earth's surface. At the equator at noon, when the Sun is directly overhead, there is more than enough energy falling on every square metre to supply about ten 100-watt light bulbs. Of the energy that arrives at the planet Earth, approximately 30 per cent is reflected back into space by the atmosphere, while 12 per cent or so is absorbed by it. About 20 per cent causes evaporation (this starts the water cycle), 8 per cent is reflected from the ground and 30 per cent is absorbed by it and subsequently re-radiated. Less than 1 per cent drives the ocean currents, winds and plant photosynthesis.

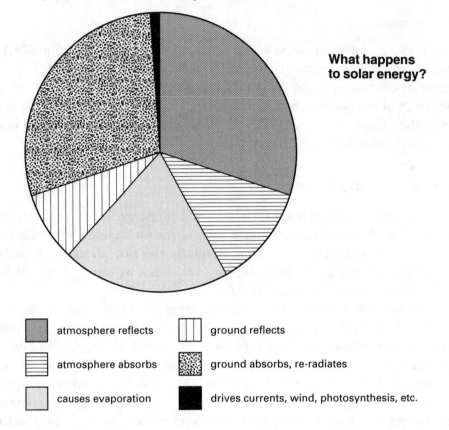

What happens to solar energy?

▦ atmosphere reflects	▥ ground reflects	
▤ atmosphere absorbs	▨ ground absorbs, re-radiates	
▢ causes evaporation	■ drives currents, wind, photosynthesis, etc.	

Solar energy gatherers fall into two main categories. Those which store the energy as heat and those which transfer it into electrical energy.

The main problem with direct solar energy is the variability. Of course, it does not work at night. Nor does it work if the Sun is hidden by clouds. Its strength is weaker in winter than it is in summer, which is a shame because most heating is naturally required in the winter. Also the further from the equator you get, the less effective solar energy becomes. One of the main drawbacks with solar energy is that too little research has gone into its development. As long as the fossil fuels are perceived to be in abundance, this is likely to remain the case.

Biomass

Strictly speaking, this is a form of solar energy, but it is large enough to merit an explanation of its own. It refers to the use of material which is provided by living organisms. The use of wood as a fuel comes into this category. In a way, this is an extension of solar energy use. Instead of storing the solar energy as heat or converting it into electrical energy, it is stored in a chemical way within the body of plant material. The Sun's rays are captured and transferred into chemical energy by photosynthesis. It is not always the plant material which is used directly in this way. Animal dung can be fermented to produce methane gas which may be used as a fuel.

More research needs to be done into this very important aspect of energy resourcing. It has been suggested that artificial photosynthesis be developed to produce simple sugars. Perhaps more realistically, bio-engineering could be employed to develop simple algae or similar plant life which has much improved photosynthetic abilities to trap sunshine and convert it into usable fuels. We will have to wait and see.

Hydroelectric power stations

As we have said, 20 per cent of the radiation from the Sun is transferred during an evaporation process. This is the source of the energy for driving the water cycle. As most people know, water is evaporated from the seas and forms clouds in the atmosphere. Under suitable conditions these clouds release their water as rain. If you think about it, not only is energy needed to convert water into water vapour, but also this water vapour is then raised up into the sky, which gives it a great increase in its potential energy. As the rain falls, this potential energy is transferred into kinetic energy.

If the rain falls on high ground such as in mountainous regions, it forms streams which contain water with some potential energy remaining. It is possible to dam these streams or rivers so that lakes are formed behind the dam. The potential energy of the water in the lake is transferred into electrical energy by turbines below the dam wall. In this way, a very tiny amount of the energy that the Sun puts into evaporation of surface water can be used as an energy source.

Other renewable sources of energy

The Sun's rays also drive the winds. Energy from the wind can be tapped directly using wind turbines ('windmills' to most of us) which generate electrical energy. The winds also cause ocean waves and there are a number of designs for devices to generate electrical energy from the waves. The current school of thought is that it is unlikely that much of the energy that we use in the future will come from such sources. There is, however, a lot of powerful vested interest in other energy industries. It is in their interests that such alternative supplies should be seen as failures. Once again, we shall see.

There is another source of energy supply which does not originate from the Sun. Everyone knows that volcanoes release huge amounts of molten lava.

Those who live in areas with deep mines may be aware that the deeper the mine is, the hotter it usually gets. The fact is that deep under the Earth's crust there is a great deal of hot material. Hot springs that are found in certain areas of the world are further evidence of this fact. Such energy sources are called **geothermal** (heat from the Earth).

Twice a day in some coastal areas the tide comes in and goes out. Huge quantities of water are caused to ebb and flow. The water at high tide has more potential energy than at low tide, simply because it is higher up. It is possible to use the energy which this water has at high tide to drive generators and transfer the energy into electrical energy.

Currently, apart from hydroelectric generators, renewable energy resources account for only a very minor part of our total energy consumption. This situation must change and change soon if we are to continue to use energy at the current rate, never mind at the projected rate of growth.

IN CONCLUSION

Attempts have been made to define energy. This is a difficult task, since we are dealing with an abstract concept – you cannot just reach out and pick up a piece of energy! It is not a substance. Instead it seems more reasonable to help define it by describing its attributes rather than attempting to say what it is. Here are some thoughts to help you come to terms with the concept of energy.

Everything we do, everything involving change that occurs – anywhere – is a result of some energy transformation. It is during energy transformations that we become aware of energy, and it is only by means of transformations that energy becomes valuable to us.

Energy is said to be conserved. We can see, perhaps, a parallel with the teaching of young children here. Children often use modelling clay pressed into different shapes and sizes to investigate conservation of volume. Only those who have grasped the idea that volume is conserved will declare that, no matter what shape the clay is pressed into, there is still the same volume present.

Energy is a bit like this, but at a much higher conceptual level. Instead of the concrete experience of modelling clay, we are left with a difficult abstract domain. No matter what transformations take place, we are still left with the same amount of energy with which we started.

Part 2

Chapter 3

Matter

INTRODUCTION

Physics has been described as the study of matter and energy and their interrelationship. In Part I energy was discussed. It is now time to turn our attention to 'matter'. This term refers to the **material of which all things are composed**. Remember that this includes gases and liquids as well as solids. Matter, if you like, is what a force acts upon.

We can look at matter on two levels. These are the microscopic and the macroscopic.

The **macroscopic** viewpoint is on a large scale. Macroscopic properties are measurable. Examples include volume, pressure and temperature. What we encounter in our day-to-day lives are the macroscopic properties of matter. We are all familiar with the rigidity of solids, the fluidity of liquids and gases, and terms like **opacity**, **flexibility**, **plasticity** and **hardness**. Such properties are, however, the result of a great many microscopic interactions which average out to produce these macroscopic effects.

A **microscopic** point of view considers things on a very much smaller scale. It is important to unite the two points of view because in the end they must lead to the same results: they must describe what we observe in the real world.

TYPES OF MATTER

Matter can be divided into two groups of materials. There are **elements** and **compounds**. It is not possible, using chemical reactions, to break an element down into anything more basic. Elements can, however, be combined chemically. These chemically bonded groups of elements are called compounds.

Hydrogen and oxygen are examples of elements. Water is a compound made up of two parts of hydrogen to one part of oxygen. (More about the size of the parts in a moment.)

Elements and atoms

Let's consider elements first. If we take a large quantity of an element, say a cupful, is it possible to keep dividing it into smaller parts for ever? Sooner or later you surely must get down to the smallest particle of the element that can exist. We call this smallest particle an **atom**. We have arrived at the microscopic world! Atoms are incredibly tiny; ten thousand million of them laid end to end would measure about a metre.

Compounds and molecules

If you try to break a compound up into smaller parts, you eventually arrive at its smallest particle, which is called a **molecule**. A molecule is made up of a number of atoms chemically bonded together. A water molecule is made up of one atom of oxygen and two atoms of hydrogen.

In order to see how the atoms of different elements differ from one another, we need to look inside an atom itself.

INSIDE THE ATOM

An atom has a fine structure. Basically, it has two distinct areas. At its centre it has a **nucleus**. Around the nucleus we find a number of tiny particles with electrical properties; these are called **electrons**. In a simplified approach to the atom, these electrons are said to orbit the nucleus in rather the same way as satellites orbit the Earth, or planets orbit the Sun.

Most of the atom is filled with empty space between the nucleus and the orbiting electrons. This is because the nucleus is tiny compared even to the tiny atom. It has less than one ten-thousandth the diameter of the atom. Even so, it is a highly complex structure. It is where nearly all the mass of the atom is concentrated. If you put two spoonfuls of concentrated nuclei in your tea instead of sugar, your tea would have more mass than two million small cars!

We could say that the nucleus is composed of two types of particle. The first is the **proton**, which like the electron has electrical properties. Electrical properties come in two 'flavours' called **positive** and **negative**. We say the proton is positive and the electron is negative.

The second of the particles in the nucleus is called the **neutron**. Neutrons

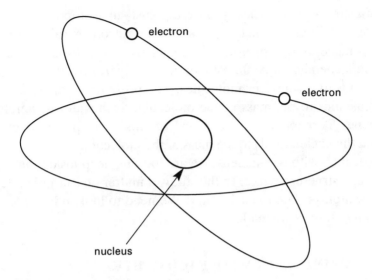

have no electrical properties and are said to be electrically **neutral**.

Atoms of *all* elements are composed of protons, neutrons and electrons. **What distinguishes one element from another is the number of protons that it has in its nucleus.** All protons are identical, as are all electrons and all neutrons. It is the *number* of protons which is important in determining the element.

Here are some examples of elements and the number of protons that they have. We call the number of protons the **atomic number** of the element.

Element	Hydrogen	Carbon	Iron	Iodine	Uranium
Number of protons	1	6	26	53	92

Hydrogen is the simplest atom, having one proton, although it is the only atom normally to have no neutrons in its nucleus. The amount of positive electricity (positive charge) held by the proton is exactly the same as the negative charge held by the electron.

In a neutral atom there is the same number of electrons in orbit as there are protons in the nucleus. It is possible for the atom to be neutral because the two types of charge can cancel each other out. Generally speaking, the more protons there are in the nucleus, the greater the number of neutrons tend to be, although there is no hard-and-fast rule about this.

You can have two atoms of the same element (that is, having the same number of protons in the nucleus) which have different numbers of neutrons. These are called different **isotopes** of the atom.

Hydrogen atoms which have a single neutron in the nucleus are called

deuterium atoms, but basically they are just an isotope of hydrogen. An isotope of hydrogen in which there are two neutrons is called **tritium**. Since deuterium has only one proton in the nucleus, it is a form of hydrogen and behaves in a chemical way almost like normal hydrogen. It will combine with oxygen atoms to form water molecules. The presence of the extra neutron in the nucleus adds to the mass of the molecule. Such water is therefore called **heavy water**. Perhaps you have heard of this? The presence of the extra neutron in the nucleus adds to the mass of the molecule.

When dealing with the nucleus, we are looking deep inside the atom to see what its basic structure is like. In the study of matter on a larger scale, we need to see how atoms relate to each other. We need to look at how atoms behave rather than how they are made.

HOW ATOMS INTERACT WITH EACH OTHER

First of all, let's look closely at the structure of the atom. We are especially interested in the outer parts, for these will determine the interaction between individual atoms. We are dealing here with the electrons, which, as we have said, can be thought of as surrounding the nucleus.

The electron is tiny even by atomic standards. It is so tiny that it has about one hundred-thousandth of the diameter of an atom. (Remember, ten thousand million atoms laid end to end would stretch about 1 metre!) Despite its diminutive size, however, the electron is very important. This is because the electron carries a negative electric charge. This means that it will be attracted to the nucleus, which carries a positive charge, because one of the rules of electricity is that unlike charges attract.

As a result of the constraints imposed by what is called **quantum mechanics**, the electron is unable to spiral in to the nucleus as you might have expected. Quantum mechanics is a highly advanced mathematical tool used by scientists to explain in detail the behaviour of electrons in atoms.

The really amazing thing is that the charge on the proton (positive) and the charge on the electron (negative) are opposite in sign but, as far as we can tell, exactly the same in strength. This is enormously important. Take the case of hydrogen, which is the simplest atom and is composed of one proton in the nucleus and one electron 'surrounding' it. It means that the atom itself is electrically neutral, since the charges on the proton and the electron exactly cancel each other out.

The picture of the atom should be becoming clearer now. At its core we have a nucleus with protons and neutrons. (Simple hydrogen is *the* exception, having no neutrons!) Surrounding the atoms are electrons, which take up most of the space in an atom and which, in comparison to the size of the nucleus, are located at great distances away. To visualize this, think of the nucleus in terms of a large pea about 1 centimetre across. The electrons would be in the surrounding space up to a distance of about a thousand metres. As you can see, the atom is mostly empty space!

Of course, these figures should not be taken too literally because the size of the nucleus is determined by the number of protons and neutrons it contains. The number of electrons is determined by the number of protons and this means that they will not all be at the same distance from the nucleus.

The way that these electrons behave is what chiefly determines the **interaction** between atoms. It is thought that there is a definite arrangement of the electrons. They seem to form **shells** around the nucleus. Each shell has a definite maximum number of electrons in it. Filled shells seem to be more stable than unfilled ones. Once a shell is filled, additional electrons have to be placed in the next available shell, further out from the centre. Complete shells always contain an even number of electrons, although not all even numbers produce complete shells.

A **neutral** atom has the same number of electrons as protons. If an electron from the outer shell of an atom is lost, the atom has one more proton than it has electrons. This leaves it with a net positive charge. Such a charged atom is called a positive ion. An **ion** in this context is a charged-up atom.

Electrons which find themselves alone in an outer shell are vulnerable to being removed from the atom, forming just such a positive ion. This holds true even though it means slightly upsetting the electrical balance. Metal atoms tend to lose their outer electrons in this way.

For example, an atom of the metallic element sodium has eleven protons in its nucleus. It therefore has eleven electrons in its neutral state. The inner shell is full with two electrons. The next shell is full with eight electrons. This leaves one electron alone in the outer shell. This electron is easily lost to produce a positive sodium ion.

Atoms of other elements, like chlorine or fluorine, have an almost full outer shell. They behave as if they have a vacancy for an electron, and readily accept free electrons to complete the shell. It is also possible for a neutral atom of this type, needing only one electron to complete its outer shell, to steal one of the electrons lost, for example, by a sodium atom. Such an atom would become a negative ion. Fluorine is an element with nine protons in its nucleus. This means that it has nine electrons in its neutral state. There are two electrons in the first shell but only seven in the outer shell. One more electron would fill this shell and render it more stable. The electron given up by the sodium atom may find its way into this vacancy. The electron finds it harder to escape this stable arrangement and so it tends to remain to form a negative fluorine ion.

Remember that a chemical compound is made of molecules which are formed when two or more atoms become bonded together. One way of achieving this bond is to allow a positive ion of sodium to attract a negative ion of fluorine to form sodium fluoride. Such a bond is called an **ionic bond**. This is not the only type of chemical bond, but it is perhaps the simplest. One thing that all bonds have in common is that they involve the electrons which surround the nucleus of the constituent atoms. In a crystal there are large numbers of sodium and fluorine ions, so large numbers of bonds exist. It is not possible to be specific about which fluorine ion any particular sodium ion is bonded to. Each positive sodium ion is surrounded by negative fluorine ions and vice versa.

Scientists tend to like to classify things. For example, we can collect some elements together and classify them as **metals**. Metals have certain physical and chemical properties in common. These properties are mainly due to their electron structure.

For example, metals tend to be good conductors of electricity. Like sodium, atoms of other metals tend to have few electrons in the outer shell. As we have seen, these electrons may easily be lost to form positive ions. This is not all, however. They are only loosely held to the atom to which they 'belong'. In fact, you might even say that in the body of the metal as a whole they do not really belong to any single atom in particular. Rather they may simply drift around in the metal from atom to atom, taking their electric charge with them. An electric current is simply a flow of charged particles, so these loosely held electrons form the basis for an electric current.

Metals are good conductors of heat energy, and this too is accounted for by the mobility of the electrons in the outer shell. As the electrons drift around they are able to carry some energy with them, which we see as heat. Similarly, this electron property is responsible for the lustre that metals have on them as they are polished. Electrons form layers in the body of a metal. This layering is responsible for the shiny effect. Metals are also well known for being malleable and ductile. Yet again, the arrangement of electrons has a part to play in these two properties.

Metals, as a family, also behave in a similar way in a chemical sense. This is because they readily form positive ions and therefore take part in ionic bonding.

The elements fluorine, chlorine, bromine and iodine also tend to behave in broadly similar ways to each other (but quite differently from the metals) in a chemical sense. They are very reactive and this is because they have a deficiency of only one electron in the outer shell. One more electron and the shell would be full. They all readily form negative ions by accepting an electron. These elements are called **halogens** by scientists.

Scientists have grouped the elements in a special way, called the **periodic table of the elements**. This classification of the elements is a consequence of the structure of the electron shells around the nucleus. By carrying out more detailed analyses of the type we have hinted at with metals and halogens, chemical properties of the elements can be predicted.

A particularly interesting group of elements are the so-called **noble** or **inert gases**. Some elements have electron shells which are completely filled, with neither any spaces nor any extra electrons. Helium is one such element. Helium has two protons in the nucleus and therefore in its neutral state it has two electrons, just enough to fill the inner shell. For this reason, helium does not readily gain or lose electrons. In fact, it does not play any significant part in chemical reactions at all. Helium is found quite alone as single unbonded atoms. Other such noble gases are neon, argon, krypton, xenon and radon.

ACIDS AND ALKALIS

Acids

Some foods or flavours have a sour taste. These are said to be **acid**. Lemons taste sour because they contain a substance called citric acid. Vinegar has a similar effect on our sense of taste because it contains acetic acid. There are many substances which chemists call acids, but it would be inconvenient, and possibly fatal, if we could identify them as acids only by their taste. You would not be wise to try tasting the sulphuric acid from a car battery!

Acids are usually thought to be corrosive. However, corrosiveness depends not only on the nature of the acid, but on the nature of what is being corroded. While the sulphuric acid in a car battery will rapidly damage clothing if accidental spillage occurs, it does not corrode the plastic casing of the battery. Imagine what would happen to your car if it did!

Corrosiveness, therefore, is not a property of the acid alone and is not a very helpful idea to use in describing acids.

Indicators

Fortunately, there are also many substances which change colour when mixed with an acid. We see such colour changes in beetroot or red cabbage when these are pickled in vinegar. Both turn to a brighter red. You could see a similar effect if you crushed a red or blue flower petal on to a piece of blotting paper and then added a drop of vinegar or lemon juice to the stain on the paper. We can use this property of colouring matter from plants to 'indicate' the presence of an acid. Such substances are called **indicators**.

Litmus is a well-known indicator extracted from a lichen. When dissolved in pure water litmus has a purple colour, but when an acid is added it will turn it red. Litmus can be used to show the presence of many acids, provided the acid is strong enough to make the litmus change colour.

In order for these colour changes to occur, the acid and/or the indicator must be dissolved in water to form a **solution**. A perfectly dry acid, such as citric acid crystals, would have no effect on dry litmus powder.

Alkalis

Some substances dissolved in water cause indicators to change to a different colour from that which is produced by acids. For example, a solution of ammonia turns litmus blue. These substances are called **alkalis**. In a sense, alkalis are the opposites of acids, and when acids and alkalis are mixed in the correct proportions, they can **neutralize** each other. The result of this neutralization will be a solution of a **salt** in water. The word 'salt' here is used in a general way to describe the substances formed by neutralization. Table salt or 'common salt' is just one of many examples.

Acids, alkalis and salts

All acids, alkalis and salts are made up of **ions**. An acid, alkali or salt is made up of positive ions and negative ions, which can, of course, attract one another. However, dissolving such substances in water frees the ions from each other. Such a solution can be thought of as containing large numbers of both positive and negative ions which are no longer bonded together.

Neutral hydrogen has only one electron, which, as is the case with metals, is easily lost to form hydrogen ions. The positive ions in acids *always* include hydrogen ions, but the negative ions can vary greatly from one acid to another.

The element oxygen has eight electrons, two in the inner shell and six in the outer shell. It therefore has the ability to accept two electrons to fill its outer shell with eight electrons and form a negative ion. It can be doubly ionized in this way to form a **doubly negative** oxygen ion. If a hydrogen atom approaches, it is possible for the outer electron of the hydrogen atom to be lost to the oxygen atom. If the oxygen atom absorbs one more electron from another source, the combination of oxygen and hydrogen atoms is singly ionized and is called a **hydroxide ion**, OH^-. The negative ions in alkalis are always hydroxide ions, but the positive ions are various, usually a metal like sodium. Thus sodium hydroxide, caustic soda, is a typical alkali.

When an acid and an alkali neutralize each other, the hydrogen ions from the acid combine with the hydroxide ions from the alkali to form water molecules. The positive ions from the alkali and the negative ions from the acid are then left in the water solution as salt. When the water is evaporated away, the positive and negative ions bond together to form salt crystals. To summarize:

Acid + Alkali $\longrightarrow$ Salt + Water

MOLECULES

When atoms of elements become bonded together in some way, they form what we call **molecules**. The molecule is the smallest particle of a compound that can exist. The simplest molecules contain only two atoms. An example of such a two-atom or **diatomic** molecule is carbon monoxide. This is a molecule made of one atom of carbon and one atom of oxygen. It is not necessary for the molecules to be made of atoms of different elements. For example, oxygen molecules are made of two atoms of oxygen bound together. In this form it is the gas needed for us to breathe. If three atoms of oxygen combine then a new gas called **ozone** is formed. You may have heard of this substance. It forms a protective layer in the upper atmosphere. It is important to us because it stops some of the Sun's harmful ultraviolet rays from reaching the surface of the Earth. Actually, if you breathe it in, it is not good for you at all!

Some molecules are more complicated than the diatomic ones that we have discussed so far. Some, like ozone, are **triatomic**. One very well-known triatomic molecule is water. You have heard, no doubt, about the famous H_2O. This means that a water molecule is made up of two atoms of hydrogen and one of oxygen.

In this way, molecules are built up from atoms. Many simple molecules are made of only a small number of atoms. We tend to think of these molecules in terms of tiny bouncy billiard balls. In fact, their shapes are often quite significantly different. Diatomic molecules form dumb-bell shapes. Carbon dioxide forms a straight line molecule with the carbon atom at the centre. On the other hand, a molecule of water forms a V-shape.

Some molecules can be very long indeed: for example, the molecules of life, such as **proteins** and **nucleic acids**. Some molecules, called **polymers**, are really made of chains of atoms. These giant molecules may be hundreds or thousands of atoms long. Polythene is one such polymer.

Plastics

Modern materials called **plastics** are composed of long-chained molecules. The structure of these materials is similar to a bowlful of spaghetti. If you try to pull a small amount of plastic material from a large conglomeration, it is similar to trying to pull a small amount of spaghetti from a large bowlful. The strands of spaghetti tend to become intertwined and you end up with a long thin knot of the stuff. Plastic materials are easy to draw into fibres. This is because the long chained molecules behave in a similar way to our strands of spaghetti.

Plastics also behave in a non-elastic (plastic) way because it is impossible for the strands to return to their original positions after they have been stretched out. Imagine trying to get the spaghetti to climb back into the bowl. Plastic and spaghetti certainly have a lot in common. Some people claim that they have eaten spaghetti that tastes just like plastic!

THE PHASES OF MATTER

Matter exists in three phases. We call these solids, liquids and gases. The three are usually clearly distinguishable. Let's begin by looking at them on the macroscopic scale.

A **solid** has a fixed shape. It does not change its shape to fill the bottom of a container as a liquid does. A **liquid** does not have a fixed shape, but it does have a fixed volume. A **gas** will not only take the shape of the container, but will expand (or contract, of course) to occupy the entire volume of its container.

Solids are able to withstand tension, compression and twist. Liquids can only withstand compression, but not twist or tension. Gases can withstand none of these. They are easily compressible.

Solids do not flow. Liquids and gases do and can both be classed as **fluids**. Gases tend to flow more easily than liquids, so we say that they have lower **viscosity**.

Solids and liquids tend to have greater densities than gases. It is difficult to be more precise because gases have such variable volumes and therefore variable densities.

So much for the macroscopic differences between solids and liquids. We will now take each in turn and discuss them in microscopic terms. It is no good having a microscopic theory which does not agree with the observed macroscopic properties of matter. It will therefore be important to see how a microscopic theory will explain the macroscopic behaviour.

Solids

You may wonder why we need to bother with a microscopic viewpoint at all. After all, if we are able to study the macroscopic properties and make predictions based on the studies, surely that is good enough. But the point is that there are certain macroscopically observed properties that are inexplicable except in microscopic terms.

One such phenomenon associated with the solid phase of matter is the existence of **crystals**. We have discussed the bonds that occur between atoms to form molecules. We have also discussed the formation of large molecules. The next step up is to talk about crystals.

Some crystals are made of only one element. This means that they are formed entirely of atoms bonded together in some way. The properties of the individual atoms are lost to some extent, and we are forced to deal with an aggregate of atoms.

Other crystals are formed from more than one element. The compound known as common salt can be formed into crystals. Salt is made of two elements, sodium and chlorine. These pairs of atoms, we could say molecules, arrange themselves to form regular crystals. If you have never done so, it is really fascinating to use a magnifying glass to take a look at some ordinary table salt. Sugar is chemically much more complicated than common salt, but it too forms crystals. If you look at granulated sugar under a magnifying glass, you can clearly see crystals.

There is no way that a macroscopic analysis can explain the existence of crystals. So just how do crystals form? To start with, let's use the billiard-ball model of the atom. This model assumes that atoms are hard spheres. When dealing with molecules we can use the same idea. If you pack balls together on a flat surface, they tend to fit together as shown in this diagram.

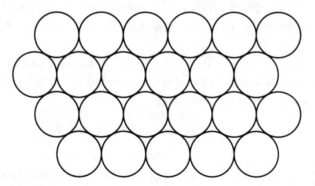

Notice the regularity of the packing. In particular, look out for the regular hexagons (six-sided figures).

Crystals are three-dimensional and the diagram above shows only a two-dimensional view. However, if you want to build up a three-dimensional model of a crystal, what you need to do is to start with the layer in the diagram and then to build up a second layer above it. The balls will naturally fall into the places shown in the following diagram. Try it with marbles or something similar if you are not sure.

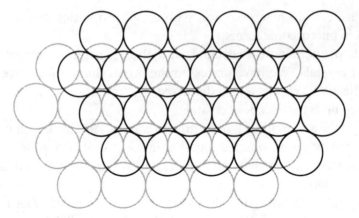

By building up layer upon layer like this, regular crystal shapes can be formed. The crystals are held together by the bonds that exist between the atoms or molecules. In fact, the same thing happens to atoms as happens to molecules in cases like these. For simplicity we will refer to molecules for now, but do bear in mind that we might just as easily be referring to atoms.

The billiard-ball model is a good one as far as it goes, but it does not take into account the fact that molecules are constantly vibrating about their mean position within the crystal. The energy that they have is constantly being swapped from kinetic to potential and back again. The situation is very similar to a child playing on a swing.

One way of forming solids is to cool a liquid. Sometimes the resulting solid may take a crystalline form. When this happens, molecules within the liquid travel around until they arrive at a suitable vacancy on a newly forming crystal.

Not all solids are crystalline, of course. Some solids, for example, form what are called **amorphous solids**. The glass that constitutes your windows is one example, and brittle toffee is another!

Liquids

Let's look at the macroscopic differences between solids and liquids and try to explain these on a microscopic scale.

Liquids have similar, although generally slightly lower, densities to solids. This should mean that the average distance between the molecules of a liquid is not very different from the solid phase. The difference between solids and liquids on a molecular level must therefore be associated more with the **arrangement** of the molecules than with their **proximity**.

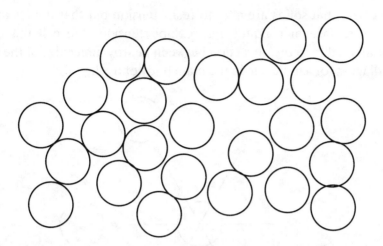

Solids maintain their shape whereas liquids flow. This statement is an oversimplification because, as you know, some solids are malleable. Metals in particular can be forged to produce different shapes. Nevertheless, when compared with liquids, solids display rigidity or stiffness.

Think about what 'flowing' means at the molecular level. It might be helpful to think about 'pouring' materials like table salt. The salt grains are tiny and they are able to move relative to each other. They give the appearance of flowing like a liquid. There is a difference between the molecules of a liquid and the grains of salt in that there is some degree of attraction between the molecules which is not present in the case of the salt grains. However, the principle is much the same.

Even in liquids there is a resistance to flowing. This resistance is called **viscosity**. Treacle is a good example of a viscous liquid. Water flows more easily than treacle. Motor oil is another viscous liquid. *Please note*: many people confuse viscosity with density. Motor oil will float on the surface of water, so it is less dense than water. On the other hand, it resists flowing more strongly than water, so it is more viscous.

Liquids and solids both have fixed volumes. This can be explained in terms of the average distance between the molecules remaining fixed in both cases. For the solid they have a fixed mean position; for the liquid they move around, but remain in close proximity to one another.

Solids and liquids resist compression. This is explained by the fact that the molecules are densely packed. There is not a lot of room left once the molecules are arranged in the solid, and much the same can be said of the liquid. Although there is a force which holds molecules together if they are close enough, there is another, even shorter-range force of repulsion which prevents them from getting too close! This repulsive force is very important, since without it matter would simply collapse in on itself.

We have said that solids are able to resist tension but that liquids are not. Actually the surface of a liquid *does* exhibit tension. We call this **surface tension**. It arises due to the attraction between nearby molecules of the liquid. Here is a diagram of a molecule in the main body of the liquid.

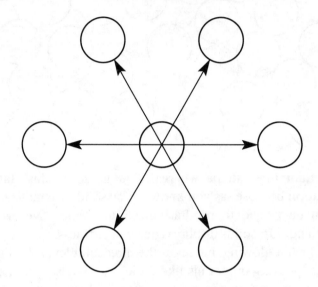

As you can see, it is surrounded by other molecules. This means that it has intermolecular forces acting upon it in all directions. The effects of these forces cancel out. The result is that the molecule is free to move around the bulk of the liquid unhindered by these forces, although there are likely to be a larger number of collisions between it and nearby neighbours, which results in a greater resistance to motion.

Now here is a diagram of the surface of a liquid.

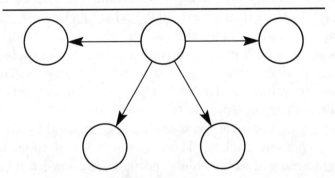

As you can see, there is now an imbalance in the effects of the intermolecular forces. The lateral forces still cancel out, but the vertical forces do not. Sure enough there is a downward force attracting the molecule back into the main body of the liquid, but there is a distinct absence of upward force to counter this effect.

Now think about a water droplet. In particular, think about the forces acting on the molecules on the surface. Can you see how a droplet can be held together? Here is a diagram to help! (It shows the forces on the outer molecules only.) As you can see, there is a force acting at the surface which always acts towards the centre of the drop. It is this which holds the drop together.

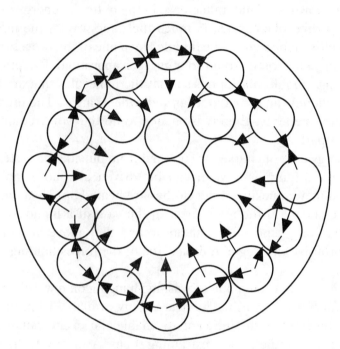

Surface tension causes liquids to act as though they have a skin on the surface. Some insects, like pondskaters, use this 'skin' to support their bodies as they move around on ponds and rivers. Detergents act to seriously weaken surface tension. If you try forming water droplets on top of a greased surface, you will find that they change spectacularly if you touch them with a wire dipped in detergent.

If you try to remove a molecule from the surface of the liquid, you can see that you have to overcome the force that pulls it back into the bulk of the liquid. Remember that, if you move against a force, you are doing work. This means that you have to put energy into the system to remove a molecule from a liquid. (This applies to any molecule in the liquid, since all molecules must pass through the surface if they are to escape.) Another way to look at this is to regard the forces between molecules as bonds. Each line showing a force in the diagrams represents a bond. It requires energy to break these bonds.

This effect is quite a significant one. It means that, in order to liberate the molecules from a liquid (that is, to vaporize it or turn it into a gas), you need to put in energy. This energy goes into breaking the bonds between the molecules. It does not go into *kinetic energy* of the molecules at all. Rather, what we are really doing is giving the molecules *potential energy*.

If you find this difficult to conceive at first, think about it in another context. Think of a rocket escaping from the clutches of the Earth's gravity. Here large amounts of fuel are needed. The energy stored in this fuel is eventually transferred into an increase in the potential energy of the rocket as it moves off into deep space, in much the same way as the molecule moves away from the main body of the liquid. The name of the process where there is a change in state from a liquid to a gas is **evaporation.** The process concerns the breaking of molecular bonds so that the molecules that are held together tightly in a liquid can spread out far and wide as a gas. The breaking of these bonds requires energy. Energy is needed to do the work required to pull the molecules apart.

This energy can, of course, be supplied from outside the system. Think of a pile of wet washing. The water can be 'driven off' more rapidly – that is, evaporated more quickly – if the clothes are heated up. Heat energy increases the kinetic energy of the molecules. In the case of a liquid they are moving around relatively gently. Heat them up and they move around a great deal more vigorously, and begin to break free of the forces holding them together as a liquid.

Now think of that same pile of washing hanging on a washing line. Suppose it is still hot from the wash. The heat energy available from the hot water in the wet clothes may be sufficient to enable the excited molecules to eject themselves free of the forces restraining them. As a result, the washing loses water and cools down.

Now consider some washing put out to dry which is at the *same temperature* as the air outside. Does it dry? Does the water turn to a gas? We must be careful here, since temperature is not the only factor at work: the presence of wind also has a significant effect. Perhaps curiously, the washing will still dry out, albeit more slowly.

The water has *some* heat energy in it. It is not freezing, for example. Thus the water molecules are able to move around. Molecules do not all have the same speed. Some move more slowly than the average; some move more quickly. The quicker molecules have more kinetic energy and so are able to break free. This leaves the slower molecules. The least energetic – that is to say, the coolest – are left behind. In other words, heat energy is lost. The washing cools down, and moreover it even cools below the temperature of the surrounding air.

You may have seen this explained in books as 'evaporation causes cooling'. Perhaps this is slightly better expressed as **cooling – that is, loss of latent heat energy – occurs as a result of evaporation.**

Does evaporation occur only on washing lines? Washing lines are certainly a good example, for the greater the surface area presented to the air here, the greater the opportunity for evaporation. Wet washing left in a pile on the floor will take a very long time to dry indeed! But evaporation can occur in any situation where a liquid has a free surface, such as where it meets a gas, and where there is sufficient energy available to enable detachment of the liquid molecules. Even a jar of water standing in a cool, dark room will slowly lose the liquid to the surroundings. Again, molecules at the relatively small surface in contact with the air are able to break free.

The heat energy needed to cause a liquid to evaporate is given the name **latent heat.** This is because if you supply heat to the liquid, as by boiling a kettle, the temperature of the liquid can be maintained while it evaporates. A boiling kettle is always at 100 °Celsius. The vapour which is given off in this heating process is at the same temperature as the liquid from which it escaped. The steam above a kettle is also at 100 °Celsius. In this way the heat is hidden, since it is not accompanied by a change in temperature, hence the name.

There is also latent heat associated with a change from a solid to a liquid. The regular arrangement of the molecules in a solid means that the number of bonds that exist is larger than exists in the liquid phase. This means that some of the bonds need to be broken when converting a solid into a liquid (**melting**). This requires energy in the same way as evaporation. The number of bonds broken during melting is much less than during evaporation, where *all* the bonds need to be broken, so the latent heat associated with melting is much less than that associated with evaporation. Nevertheless, latent heat exists here as well. That is why it is more effective to put ice at 0 °Celsius into your drink to cool it than it is to put the same amount of water at 0 °Celsius. The water contains a lot of potential energy due to the broken bonds that the ice does not have.

Gases

Gases have much lower densities than either solids or liquids; and they are highly compressible. The molecules in a gas behave in a totally different way to those in solids and liquids. The main difference is that in a gas the molecules are, on average, much farther apart than in a solid or a liquid. In fact, to a large extent we can ignore the intermolecular attractions between molecules.

In a gas, molecules are in continuous random motion. They therefore have a certain amount of kinetic energy.

Before we go into more detail about the behaviour of molecules in a gas, we really need to consider the macroscopic behaviour of gases themselves. To start with, it is necessary to think about the attributes that a gas may have. For a given amount of gas (by 'amount' here we refer to mass of gas), one of the things which interests us is the volume which the gas occupies.

As we said, gases are very easily compressed. For this reason it is not possible to state the volume of a given amount of a particular type of gas. Not, that is, unless we take the **pressure** of the gas into account.

It seems that, as you double the pressure of a gas, under the right circumstances, you can halve its volume. This relationship is found to work for many gases over a large range of pressures. Robert Boyle, a famous seventeenth-century scientist, formulated his well-known gas law around this relationship. We must still be careful, though, because pressure and volume do not make up the whole story. The temperature of the gas is equally important. The relationship between pressure and volume works only if you make sure that the temperature does not change during the process. This is what we mean by 'under the right circumstances'.

How can we cope with situations like this, where there are three variables? It seems most confusing, until you realize that, if you hold one variable constant, you can find out how the other two are related. This is the whole basis of what is called a **fair test.** If you compare two pairs of pressures and volumes at different temperatures, this is not a fair test. Only when temperature is held constant does it become fair.

Similarly, we can investigate the relationship between temperature and pressure by keeping the volume constant. If you do this, you find, not surprisingly, that as the temperature rises the pressure increases. Conversely, if you lower the temperature, the pressure decreases. If you think about it, this situation cannot go on for ever because eventually the pressure will reach zero. You cannot envisage negative pressure, so the pressure can go no lower. The temperature at which this will happen turns out to be $-273\,^\circ$Celsius. Keep this figure in mind.

If you like, you can investigate the relationship between temperature and volume with the pressure held constant. Again not surprisingly, as the temperature rises the volume increases. Conversely, if you lower the temperature, the volume decreases. This situation cannot go on for ever either because eventually the volume will reach zero. Just as with pressure, you cannot have a negative volume, can you? The temperature at which this will happen also turns out to be $-273\,^\circ$Celsius. This cannot be a coincidence surely!

No, it is not a coincidence. It seems as if we have found some minimum temperature below which it is not possible to go. We call this temperature

absolute zero. We are now getting closer to the fundamental concept of temperature.

The relationships between the pressure, volume and temperature of a fixed mass of gas are so important that they are raised to the position of laws and are known collectively as the **gas laws.** Let us now examine these laws using a microscopic point of view.

First of all, what is meant by the *volume* of a gas? This does not have the same meaning as the volume of a solid or of a liquid. Liquids change their shapes but not their volumes when they are transferred from one container to another. Gases expand (or contract) to take up the volume of the container.

We need to look at what the molecules of a gas are doing. They are in continuous random motion. This means that each molecule is moving through space in a straight line until either it collides with one of its neighbours or else it collides with one of the walls of the container in which it finds itself.

The collisions with the walls and the other molecules are called **elastic collisions.** This means that there is no loss of kinetic energy during each collision. Since the walls of the container do not move during or after each collision, the molecules bounce off with the same speed as they had on impact. Elastic collisions are a bit special. They are rarely met on a large scale, but they do exist here.

How do we explain *pressure* in a gas using molecules? Did you know that in 1 litre of air bottled at 0 °Celsius there are nearly twenty-seven thousand million molecules? This means that at any time there are many collisions collisions taking place between the molecules and the walls of the container. The container walls experience a steady pressure as the forces of all the impacts are averaged out. If the pressure of the gas we have been considering is the same as that of the atmosphere, it will produce the same downward force on a 1-square-metre plank of wood as if there were 100,000 apples sitting on it.

Now for that question! What about *temperature?* Think for a moment about how the pressure of your gas could be reduced to zero. Pressure results from the collisions between the molecules and the walls of the container. If the collisions stopped then so would the pressure. The collisions would stop if the molecules stopped moving! Think about how the volume of the gas would reduce to zero. If all the molecules stopped moving around and settled to the bottom of the container, how much space would they take up? The answer is that they would take up practically zero space because molecules are very small indeed.

In this condition, the molecules would be right up against one another. Can you think what we would call molecules like this? Yes, a liquid. So temperature is connected with the *movement* of the molecules.

How do you make the temperature of a gas increase? One way is to warm it up: in other words, you supply energy. What happens to this energy on a molecular scale? The answer is that it is the source of energy which enables the kinetic energy of the molecules to increase.

Is this all? Not quite, because you will recall that gas molecules have a great deal of potential energy that liquid molecules do not have. This is due to the breaking of the intermolecular bonds. When we talk of **heat** we are referring to the *total* energy of all the molecules. **Temperature** is to do with the *kinetic* energy only.

If you put a thermometer into some boiling water, it will give you the same reading as if you placed it in some newly formed steam because both are at 100 °Celsius. In the steam, the molecules have more potential energy but the same amount of kinetic energy. Suppose you scald your finger. It is less harmful to scald it in boiling water than in steam. The temperature of each is the same, but steam contains a greater quantity of energy which can be transferred to the finger to do the damage.

The final point about temperature is that the kinetic energy we are talking about has to be averaged over all the molecules.

> **Temperature is a measure of the average kinetic energy of the molecules. Heat is a measure of the total energy of the molecules, both potential and kinetic.**

THE NUCLEUS

So far, we have seen that within an atom the number of protons will determine the type of matter we are dealing with. We have also seen that the numbers of electrons can be altered. In a neutral atom there will be the same number of protons as electrons. But an imbalance here will result in the formation of **positive or negative ions.** Remember, too, that the number of neutrons in a nucleus can vary, giving us isotopes.

Next let's look at **radioactivity.** Radioactivity comes from the nucleus of the atom. We find from observations that for any element the ratio of the number of protons to neutrons in the nucleus often seems to lie within a particular range. The value of this range varies from element to element. **If the ratio is found to be outside of these limits then the nucleus becomes unstable.** In an effort to regain stability and to get back to a permitted ratio of protons to neutrons, material will be ejected from the nucleus. This material forms the basis of radioactivity.

The ejected material is not randomly composed. Most commonly, so-called alpha or beta particles are given off. Sometimes we see neutrons. In addition to these particles, a burst of high-energy electromagnetic radiation called a gamma ray is frequently given off.

Alpha particles are quite simply made up of a pair of protons and a pair of neutrons bound together. This foursome is very stable. In fact, alpha particles are the same as helium nuclei. Because of the presence of protons they are positively charged. Alpha particles are much heavier, about eight thousand times heavier, than electrons. They interact strongly with matter that they meet. For this reason, alpha particles are easily absorbed by matter and would be unable to pass through more than a few centimetres of ordinary air. Alpha particles are most dangerous if they are ejected by atoms that you have swallowed or breathed in.

Beta particles are fast-moving electrons. They are more penetrating than the alpha particles and can pass through thin layers of light metals. This means that they can pass into the human body through the skin. They are also most dangerous if the atoms from which they are emitted find their way inside the body.

Gamma rays are the only true radiation involved with radioactivity. They are very penetrating and can pass through thick concrete walls. The thicker the wall, the less the radiation manages to find its way through. It is perfectly possible for some of the burst of gamma radiation to pass straight through the body. Usually, though, some of that burst will be absorbed and do some damage.

All types of radioactivity come under the heading of ionizing radiations. They are so called because one of the effects that they have on matter is to affect the electron structure of the atom, causing ions to form. This can have a devastating effect on living tissue.

Nuclear fission

During nuclear reactions, as you would expect, energy is transferred. There are two main nuclear processes that are of interest in this context. These are **nuclear fission** and **nuclear fusion.**

In the process of nuclear fission, heavy elements with large numbers of protons and neutrons are broken apart to form lighter elements. Currently, our nuclear power stations employ nuclear fission reactors.

In a fission reactor a heavy element like uranium is split up into smaller chunks. Each of these chunks forms the nucleus of a *lighter* element, such as caesium. In this way, the old alchemists' dream of 'transmutation of the elements' has been achieved. We may not be able to change lead into gold, but we can change the basic structure of matter.

Uranium is an example of a *heavy* element because it has a large number of protons and neutrons in its nucleus. In fact, it has 92 protons, whereas caesium, on the other hand, has only 55 protons.

In the case of lighter elements like helium, oxygen and nitrogen, the number of protons and neutrons in the nucleus is roughly the same. Helium, for example, has two protons and two neutrons, and the most commonly found form of carbon has six protons and six neutrons. Heavy elements tend to have significantly more neutrons than protons.

A common isotope of uranium known as U235 has 92 protons but 143 neutrons. (The convention which defines this as uranium isotope 235 is found from adding the 143 neutrons and the 92 protons.) From this you can see that it is an isotope then with 51 more neutrons than protons. Naturally occurring uranium is actually a mixture of the isotopes U235 and U238, which, of course, has 146 neutrons.

U235 more readily undergoes fission than U238, so the proportion of the isotope U235 in naturally occurring uranium needs to be increased. This process is called **enriching.** What we are doing here is concentrating the U235 by reducing the amount of U238.

In order to cause a U235 nucleus to fission, it has to be struck by a neutron. This very rapidly disintegrates into two much smaller daughter nuclei. There are usually a few free neutrons in existence which can be used to start the process off. The process of fission also produces two or even three *extra* neutrons. These can be used to start off further fission reactions and so the process continues. This is what is known as a **chain reaction.**

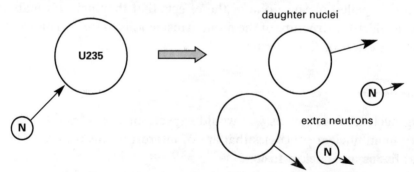

The effectiveness of these extra neutrons is increased by making them pass through a material which is said to **moderate** the neutrons and is thus called a moderator. Graphite is often used as a moderator.

The key to the whole process is the neutrons. The presence of only *one* neutron is enough to get the process started. The more of them there are, the faster the fission process takes place. In a nuclear reactor it is necessary to make sure that each fission gives rise to only one following fission in order to maintain a steady reaction rate. If you did not ensure this, the process would continue increasing, producing more and more energy at an ever-increasing rate until all the uranium was fissioned (an atom bomb is in fact just such an uncontrolled nuclear explosion).

This means that any unwanted neutrons produced have to be absorbed. This is the job of the **control rods.** These are made of a neutron-absorbing material like cadmium or boron. These can absorb neutrons safely without becoming unstable like uranium.

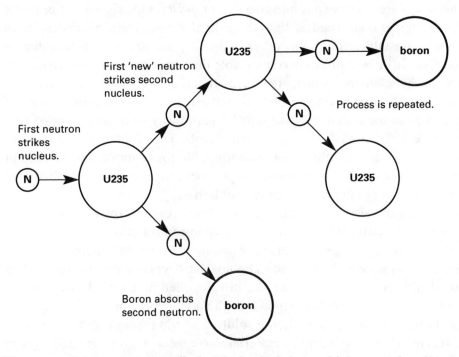

The core of the reactor usually has holes in it into which control rods may be inserted. If the reaction is running too fast, the rods may be inserted further into the core. If the reaction needs speeding up, the rods are withdrawn a little.

In addition to control rods, there are additional control rods known as **shut-down rods.** When these are inserted they absorb so many neutrons that it is impossible for the reaction to continue. In this way, the reaction may be virtually switched off. When they are withdrawn, however, the reaction may continue and build up until the control rods are used to set the rate of the reaction.

There are many types of reactor design. The main differences between them are related to the means by which the heat energy generated during the fission process is removed from the reactor core and is passed to the generators to produce electricity.

In a fast-breeder reactor U238 undergoes neutron capture and we end up, at the end of a complex process, with plutonium. This can be extracted at special nuclear-reprocessing plants. The separated plutonium can be used as a nuclear fuel and in weapon production.

Nuclear waste

As we have seen, in the process of nuclear fission the heavy nuclei of uranium or plutonium are usually split into two lighter nuclei. One significant problem as far as this is concerned is that these lighter nuclei are produced in an inherently unstable state. In other words, they are themselves highly radioactive. In an attempt to become stable they emit radiation and change to nuclei of other elements, which are, more often than not, also radioactive.

For each of these products of fission there is an internationally agreed period of time for which they have to be kept away from humanity so that their radioactivity can be reduced to 'safe' levels. The problem is that some of these time periods are rather long. Strontium 90, for example, has to be kept for over 500 years! The more waste we produce, the greater the problem we are presenting to our great-great-grandchildren.

Nuclear waste is not only produced as a direct result of the fission process. The radioactive particles emitted during fission can contaminate the coolants and other materials so that they also become dangerously radioactive.

There is also what is considered to be **low-activity waste** produced, which is disposed of by discharge into the sea in controlled amounts. In the case of gaseous wastes these are discharged into the atmosphere in a 'safe' way. The longer-lasting liquid waste is often a solution of the fission products in nitric acid. It is possible to convert this material into a solid glassy form so that it can be contained more safely. This process is called **vitrification.**

One of the problems with highly active waste is that it generates heat by similar processes to the original reactor processes. This heat has to be dissipated by passing coolants over the waste. Much waste is currently stored in concrete waste farms.

Nuclear fusion

Fusion is the opposite process to fission. In fission, heavy nuclei are split up into lighter ones. In fusion, lighter nuclei are used as building bricks to produce heavier ones.

When heavy nuclei – that is, those with large numbers of protons and neutrons – split up to form lighter nuclei, energy is given out. It is this energy which we seek to use in nuclear power stations. The splitting process, however, does not always give energy out.

For elements lighter than iron (which has 26 protons), the energy equation is reversed. From now on if you wish to fission the nuclei still further, you have to put energy *in*. The converse is also true. For elements lighter than iron, if you can get *fusion* to take place, you can get energy *out*.

Element	Hydrogen	Carbon	Iron	Iodine	Uranium
Number of protons	1	6	26	53	92

	←——————————————→		←———→	←——————————————→	
	In this range, fusion gives energy out and fission takes energy in.		Turning-point	In this range, fusion takes energy in and fission gives energy out.	

This means that it is possible to produce energy from nuclear reactions in a totally different way from that which we have been discussing so far: by nuclear fusion.

Do you remember the isotopes of hydrogen? A hydrogen nucleus is simply a single proton; deuterium has one proton and one neutron; tritium has one proton and two neutrons. Among the nuclear fusion processes that we know about is that where two deuterium nuclei are fused to produce a light isotope of helium (with two protons and one neutron) together with a single neutron; and that which produces tritium plus hydrogen. Alternatively, we could fuse deuterium with tritium to produce normal helium and a neutron. We could also try fusing deuterium with light helium to produce normal helium plus hydrogen.

Apart from the neutrons, the nuclear waste problem is minimal in fusion as compared with fission reactors. The snag is that, in order to get the fusion to happen, temperatures of around 20 million °Celsius are required!

No ordinary material could hold gases that hot, so instead a **magnetic confinement** (this is a kind of force field) is used. At such high temperatures, the electrons on the outside of the atoms of hydrogen and helium are stripped off. What we have left is described as a **plasma.** Fast-moving charged particles can be affected by magnetic fields – a kind of 'magnetic bottle' arrangement is being experimented with. The most promising is called the Tokamak system.

The Sun, in common with all stars, is in reality a giant nuclear reactor which is based on nuclear fusion. The force field that holds the Sun together is based on gravity. We could say, therefore, that we already rely on nuclear fusion for our energy supply.

Chapter 4

Electricity and Magnetism

INTRODUCTION

Electricity is generally considered in terms of electric circuits that use either batteries or mains supplies. Magnetism is often thought of in terms of bar magnets, and the link with electricity is often not appreciated. It is one of the great achievements of modern physics that these two apparently different phenomena have been linked so closely together.

Before embarking on a study of current electricity it is necessary to look deeper at the meaning of electricity itself. This means that we have to begin at the beginning with **electrostatics**.

ELECTROSTATICS

When most people talk about static electricity, they usually only talk of 'static'. Every day you are quite likely to encounter static.

Perhaps you have 'fly-away' or very fine hair. If so, you will notice how a plastic comb crackles when you use it soon after your hair has been freshly washed and dried. Quite often when this happens your hair almost stands on end as strands of it try to push each other away.

If you have any old black vinyl long-playing records, you will know how dust is attracted to them by static.

Next time you are wearing a nylon jumper or other clothing made from artificial fibres and are preparing to undress, try being extra modest and turn the lights out as well as closing the curtains. You may well see blue flashes of static as you remove your jumper. You may have already noticed the crackling sound that you make when removing clothes like these. Nylon slips are notorious for 'sticking' to other garments because of static.

If you have not noticed any of these things, perhaps you have played the game where you rub a plastic pen on a sleeve to get it to pick up tiny pieces of paper. Or you may have been unfortunate and received a painful shock as you have touched a metal door handle after walking on a man-made carpet in a dry air-conditioned office. All these are examples of static electricity.

On closer observation, it appears that there are forces acting between these objects. We say the bodies which experience such electrical forces are **electrically charged.** These are not always forces of attraction – you are just as likely to notice repulsion. If you look more closely, you will see that there are two classes of charged body.

A body of one class will repel all other bodies in its own class and attract all bodies in the other class. To make it easier, we call one class of objects **positively** charged and the other **negatively** charged. (Actually there is nothing intrinsically negative about one type of charge. We do not mean that there is something missing in negative charge that is present with positive charge. We could just as easily have swapped the names around. In fact, as you will see later, it would have been better if we had done just that!)

We can now summarize what we have found out about the forces which act between charged bodies.

Like charges repel – like the fine strands of hair pushing each other apart.

Unlike charges attract – like the dust sticking to the record. This means that the dust and the record are of opposite charge.

These are known as **the laws of electrostatics.**

But what exactly is 'charge'?

Charge is a property of bodies which allows them to feel the attraction and repulsion of electric forces. The stronger the charge on a body, the stronger will be the electrical force it will feel. The strength of charge which a body carries may be increased by 'charging it up' or decreased by 'discharging it'. The strength of charge on a body can be quantified using the idea of the strength of the force it feels.

The concept of electrical charge is fundamental to the structure of matter. We have already met this idea in Chapter 3. Remember, all matter is made of atoms. Atoms contain a nucleus which is made of two major particles, the proton and the neutron.

The proton carries a positive charge. The neutron is neutral, which means that it carries no charge. The outer parts of the atom consist of **negatively charged electrons**, which are attracted to the positive nucleus by the electric force we have just met.

An ordinary atom will, overall, be electrically neutral. The size of the positive charge on a proton exactly balances that of the negative charge on an electron. The effects of the two charges cancel out, leaving the atom apparently uncharged. When we say that a large body, made of a great many atoms, is **uncharged**, what we mean is that the total amount of positive charge is exactly balanced by the negative charge.

When something becomes positively charged, it has had this balance upset and there is an excess of positive charge over the negative. This can happen in one of two ways. Either more positive charge is added or else some negative charge is removed.

In the case of the charged pen, the imbalance in charges was achieved by the process of rubbing the pen on the sleeve. At the time of the early experiments with static electricity, plastics were not available so tests were carried out on a substance called ebonite rubbed with fur and on glass rubbed with silk. It turned out that the ebonite was given a negative charge whereas the glass was given a positive charge.

The sign of the charge depends upon the material being rubbed, although the material which does the rubbing also has an effect. Polythene becomes negatively charged when it is rubbed, and cellulose-acetate gains a positive charge.

During the rubbing process, charge is transferred either from the rubber to the rubbed or vice versa. To find out just what is going on here, we need to look again at atoms. The positive charge is held in the nucleus at the centre; the negative charge, on the other hand, is held by the electrons on the outside. When charge is transferred, it is nearly always the electrons which carry this charge.

When polythene is rubbed, it has electrons transferred to its surface and thus gains a negative charge. Acetate, on the other hand, has electrons removed from its surface and is left with an overall positive charge.

You may very well ask if all materials can be charged up in this way. Suppose you held a rod of iron in your hand and rubbed it with a cloth of some sort. Would it pick up a charge? The answer is that it would not. There is a fundamental difference between the electrical properties of materials such as iron, copper and other metals, and the electrical properties of such materials as polythene, acetate, glass and ebonite. Electrons are able to move about within the body of metals. This is not the case with polythene, for example. Here the electrons which are given to the polythene when it is charged remain on its surface where they were deposited. They are unable to move around.

> **Materials such as iron which allow electrons to flow within them are called electrical conductors.**

☐   **Materials such as polythene which do not allow electrons to flow within them are called insulators.**

When you try to place charge on the outside of a metal conductor, it simply flows through the body of the conductor and then through your body to the ground. (We will discuss this affinity for charge to find ground later on.) Only in the case of the insulator does the charge stay where it is, on the surface, and cause the body to become 'charged'.

Is it possible to charge a conductor then? Surprisingly, yes it is! Suppose a metal object is placed on a thick insulating mat. This mat would prevent any charge finding its way to ground. This means that any charge that the conductor was given would stay with it. In fact, the charge would not reside on the surface of the conductor, but would even itself out in some way throughout the material.

Unlike insulators, conductors are not usually charged by rubbing. One way to charge up a conductor would be to place it in contact with another conductor which carries some charge. In this case, the charge is simply shared out between the two. But how did the charge get on the second conductor in the first place?

A better method of charging conductors is by a process called **induction.** This term is often used in science. It describes the kind of process where an action is taken which results in a secondary effect. It is this secondary effect which is said to be 'induced'.

Picture a rod of iron. Imagine that you brought a positively charged piece of acetate near to one end of the rod. The electrons in the rod would be attracted to the end nearest the acetate. This would leave the other end with a deficiency of electrons. We say that a charge has been induced on either end of the rod. If the rod were now connected to the ground, some electrons from the ground would rush into the rod to make up for the deficiency in the end away from the acetate. If the connection to ground is now removed, the electrons are trapped. The acetate may now be removed. The newly acquired electrons spread throughout the rod, which has become negatively charged. The way that the electrons arrange themselves within the body of a conductor is a little strange and is worth remarking on. It seems that charge accumulates at a sharp part of the surface. The strength of the electric force is greater at sharp points.

This can be really useful. One dramatic natural demonstration of what happens when the build-up of electric charge becomes too great is that of lightning. The charge which accumulates in clouds rather enthusiastically leaps to ground. It might just be that your church steeple, or a tall factory chimney, is the highest point in the area and that the lightning would strike

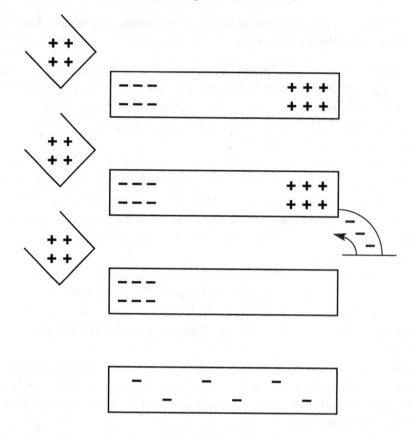

here. You want to avoid a direct strike if you can. To help with this a device called a **lightning conductor** is attached. This is simply a thick band of copper (copper is a good conductor) that has a spike at the top to attract the lightning, and is firmly embedded in the ground at the other end. The charge on the clouds induces an opposite charge at the spike of the lightning conductor. This is because, as we have said, charge builds up at a point. The lightning then travels through the conductor to the ground instead of attacking the church steeple.

Incidentally, this is why you should *never* use an umbrella in a thunderstorm. In effect you are carrying your own personal lightning conductor, except that the handle is not connected to the ground directly – *it is connected to the ground through you!*

POTENTIAL DIFFERENCE

So far we have considered electricity in terms of electric charge. We are aware of the presence of charge because of the electric forces that act between charged objects. Before we investigate electricity any further, we need to recap on potential energy.

You will recall that sometimes a body may have a store of energy and that this is called **potential energy** because it has the potential to be transferred and thus be involved in changes that take place.

One common form of potential energy is **gravitational potential energy.** If you pull against gravity to lift an object above the ground, you give it potential energy. You have had to do work to supply this energy. (Remember, energy cannot be created or destroyed.) You have had to move the object upwards against the force of gravity, which acts downwards. This work is transferred into potential energy. If you release the object after you have lifted it, the force of gravity will cause it to fall. It will gain kinetic energy as it falls, but it will lose the potential energy that you gave it.

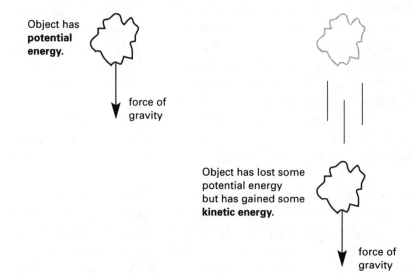

Now, we move from thinking about the force due to gravity and think about electrical forces. Think about this example. Two large flat metal plates are placed horizontally one above the other, separated by a distance of 200 mm or so (20 cm to you and me). The top plate is given a positive charge and the bottom is given a negative one. A light ball of plastic is given a positive charge and is held near the top plate, as shown in this diagram.

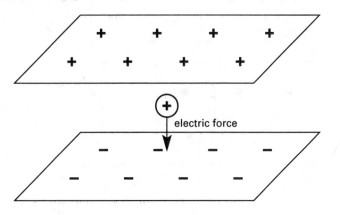

Think about the electric forces acting on the light ball. Incidentally, we have decided to use a light ball so that the electric forces are considered to be much greater than the force of gravity. In this way we can ignore the force of gravity – we are only dealing here with electrical forces. Of course, we could equally well be talking about protons, which are very light balls indeed! Electrons would behave in a similar way, but the forces they would feel would be in the other direction because they are negatively charged. The ball and the top plate are both positively charged and like charges repel. The ball and the bottom plate are of opposite charge and unlike charges attract.

The net effect is to produce a downward force on the ball. Consider what would happen to the ball if it were to be released. It would begin moving towards the bottom plate. It would increase its kinetic energy. The question that needs to be answered now is, just where did this kinetic energy come from? There must have been some store of energy. The ball at the starting point has more potential energy than it has when it reaches the bottom plate. The idea is exactly the same as the concept of gravitational potential energy, except that here we are talking about electrical potential energy.

The ball has a different amount of potential energy when it is near the top plate and when it is near the bottom plate. It has changed position and this has changed its potential energy. There is obviously something special about the space between the plates.

The charged ball will experience an electric force if it is placed in this region. What is special about this region is that it is **one in which an electric force can be felt.** Scientists give such a region a special name. It is called a **force field.** In the case of the two plates, the field is an electrical one. Correspondingly, in the case of regions near the Earth where there is a force of gravity to be felt, we say that such regions are in a gravitational force field.

We represent force fields diagrammatically by drawing lines which have arrows on them. These arrows indicate the direction of the force that would be felt by a body with a positive charge.

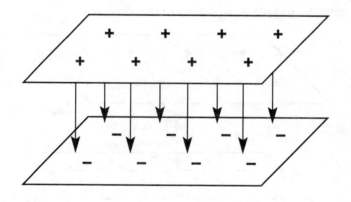

The existence of force fields is fundamental to the study of physics. As far as we are concerned, we need to see the link between potential energy and force fields. If you move around within a force field, it is possible that you will change your potential energy.

For example, in the case of the ball between two plates that we have been looking at, if the movement is at *right angles* to the field (horizontal movement) then there is no work done and the energy of the ball does not change.

If the movement is *against* the arrows then work has to be done against the force field and the potential energy of the ball is increased.

If the movement is in the *same direction* as the arrows then there is work done by the force field and the potential energy of the ball is decreased.

In the case of the field between parallel plates, it does not matter whereabouts the ball is placed. It will always feel the same force. The field is said to be **uniform.**

There is a difference between gravitational fields and electric fields. Gravitational forces between two bodies are always attractive. In the electric case there are two types of charge. If the ball in the example above had been negatively charged, like the electron, instead of positively charged, the whole situation would have been reversed. The force on the ball would have been upwards instead of downwards.

This leads us to ask, just which way should we draw the arrows on the field diagram? It has been decided that, to avoid confusion, the arrows indicate the direction of the force on a body with a *positive* charge. You will need to remember that a body with a *negative* charge feels a force in the opposite direction to the arrows.

In considerations of force fields and potential energy, it is important to know just how large the force will be, and to know by just how much the potential energy of a body will change if it moves from one place to another. The answer is that it depends upon the amount of the charge that you are dealing with. In our case, this is how much charge we placed upon our ball, perhaps by scraping off electrons!

This means that, if you want to know how strong a force the field causes the ball to feel, or how large the change of potential energy will be as you move from one place to another, you will need to have an infinite number of answers ready for all the possible amounts of charge on the ball.

Naturally this is most inconvenient. We need to know just how much charge we are dealing with. It has been internationally agreed that the unit of electrical charge shall be known as the **coulomb.** We now talk about field strength in terms of the force on a body carrying a charge of 1 coulomb.

The unit of force is the newton, of course, so we measure field strength in terms of newtons per coulomb. In other words, if a charge of 1 coulomb were placed at a point, what strength of force would it feel? If you have a charge which is twice as big, you will feel a force which is twice as big. In this way, the force on a body with *any* charge is known.

A similar thing is done with potential energy. The change in potential energy of a charged ball as it is moved between two points, A and B say, depends upon the amount of charge it carries. Once again the way around this is to state the change in potential energy of one coulomb of charge as it is moved between the two points. Instead of talking about the **potential energy of 1 coulomb difference** we shorten this to the **potential difference.** You would be justified in thinking that the unit of potential difference would be the joule (the unit of energy) per coulomb. In fact the idea of potential difference is so important to the study of electricity that it is given a special unit all of its own. You may have heard of it – it is the **volt.** It is defined as follows:

> **Two points A and B are at a potential difference of 1 volt if there is a change of potential energy of 1 joule as 1 coulomb of charge is moved between them.**

When a body is 'charged up positively', it is really having its electric potential raised (or lowered if it is negatively charged). The amount of change in potential, as measured in volts, for every extra coulomb of charge the body is given is called the **capacitance** of the body. Large bodies can take on much more charge before they have their potential raised by 1 volt than can small ones. It is a bit like the change of depth of water in a bucket for every litre of water that you pour in. A big bucket, with a big capacity, can store a greater volume of water for every extra centimetre depth than can a smaller one.

ELECTRIC CURRENTS

We have now considered static electricity and electrical potential. We did, however, mention that some materials, such as metals, are called electrical conductors because electrons are free to move within them. We will now look more closely at charge on the move.

When charged bodies such as electrons are allowed to flow (you could simply think of it as a flow of charge) through a conductor, we say that here is an electric current flowing. In simple terms, an electric current is a flow of charge in the same way as the current in a river is a flow of water. One of the differences is that in the case of the river you can see the water moving, but with electric current nothing is visible.

Think about how you would measure the flow rate of a river. One way of doing it would be to measure the speed with which the water moves. In certain circumstances this would be useful – if you wanted to know whether or not a particular boat could travel upstream, for example. But if you are interested in the *amount* of water involved, you need to think again. The way you would approach this problem is to cast an imaginary net right across the river at some point, and measure how much water flowed through your net in a given time period.

In the case of our electric current, we are not simply interested in how fast the charges move. We are interested in the amount of charge that flows down a wire, for example. We can do as we have just done in the case of the water. We can cast an imaginary net across the wire and measure the amount of charge that passes through it in a given time period. If we choose one second for our time period, we will be measuring electric current in terms of the amount of charge passing a point in our circuit in one second – in other words, the amount of coulombs per second. This is a most important and basic measurement in the study of electricity and we give it its own unit. It is called the **ampere (amp for short).**

> **When a current of 1 amp flows, 1 coulomb of charge passes a point in the conductor during every second.**

You may have heard of the terms 'AC current' and 'DC current' and wondered what is the difference.

AC stands for **alternating current** and it means that the flow of charge is constantly changing direction, first one way and then the other. The simplest way to think of it is like a bob on the end of a pendulum swinging backwards and forwards. The current in AC behaves in the same way. Mains electricity is AC.

DC stands for **direct current.** Here the current flows in one direction only and is often steady in value. The current produced by batteries is of this type.

Effects of a current

Electric current is a flow of charge through a conductor. The question arises, how can you tell if a current is in fact flowing or not? As we have already established, it is not possible to 'see' a current flowing. You have to rely on the *effects* of a current in order to detect its presence.

Think about how electric current flows through a metal wire. The wire is a solid, so you can picture it as an array of atoms vibrating about fixed positions. The outer electrons of the metal atoms are only loosely held to the atom. In fact, the bonding is so loose that it is impossible to tell just which atom the electron belongs to. According to classical physics (non-quantum mechanical), you can imagine the wire to be made of a matrix of positive ions immersed in a sea of electrons. A good analogy is to think of a sponge soaked with water. The fibres of the sponge represent the atoms and the water represents the outer, mobile electrons.

Now think about how the current is going to be caused to flow. Some way of making the electrons move from one end to the other is needed. Remember that electrons are negatively charged and will be attracted to something positive and repelled from something negative. If you arrange it so that one end of the wire is made positive and the other is made negative, you will enable the electrons to flow away from the negative end and towards the positive one.

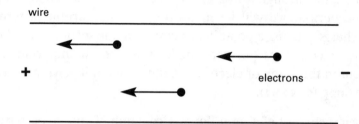

How can this be achieved? In order to get electrons to move, you need to give them kinetic energy. The system must be supplied with energy. What you need to do is provide a source of electrical potential energy by applying a potential difference to the ends of the wire. The source of energy for the flow of electrons is a potential difference.

> **The first thing that is needed for a current to flow continuously is a potential difference.**

This means that the electrons are attracted to one end of the wire by a force. Remember, a force can cause a body to move faster. The electrons would continue to gain kinetic energy at the expense of electrical potential energy, and get faster and faster. There is, however, a snag. The electrons do not get very far before atoms get in their way. When a tiny electron strikes a large atom, the effect is rather like firing a grain of rice at a cannon ball. The electron bounces off and loses some of its kinetic energy. The atom gains this energy and begins to vibrate about its position with a little more vigour. Every collision causes the atom to gain just a little more energy.

From the position of an outside observer, the wire is seen to get hotter. The electrical energy of the potential difference is transferred into electric current energy – that is, kinetic energy of the electrons – and this ends up as heat energy in the wire unless the energy is transferred to some other form by a device like an electric motor.

One effect of an electric current, therefore, is that it causes heating. The overall effect in energy terms is that a source of electrical potential energy is supplied and this is transferred into heat.

Let's go back to thinking about our piece of wire again. If one end of it is made positive and the other negative, the electrons will tend to flow away from the negative end and towards the positive end. Think about the consequences of this for a moment.

The negatively charged electrons will tend to counteract the positive charge of the positive end of the wire. Equally important, the lack of electrons in the negative end offsets the negative charge that was put there. Eventually, both ends will become neutral again and the current will stop.

How do we ever get a current to flow then? The answer is that, once the electrons arrive at the positive end of the wire, they must be removed somehow. Meanwhile, at the negative end, electrons need to be supplied in order to make up for those that have drifted away.

The problem is that the electrons at the positive end are attracted there, and work needs to be done to remove them. Similarly, the electrons are repelled from the negative end, and to place some there requires that work is done. This is the job of the battery. It has a positive terminal and a negative terminal. Each end of the wire is connected to a terminal. The electrons in the wire are attracted to the positive terminal. The battery contains stored energy in a chemical form. This energy is used to remove the electrons from the positive terminal and to place them on the negative terminal connected to the other end of the wire. From here the electrons begin their travels through the wire once again. What we have here is a complete circuit. Without a complete circuit the current will soon come to a halt.

The second thing that is needed for a current to flow continuously is a complete circuit.

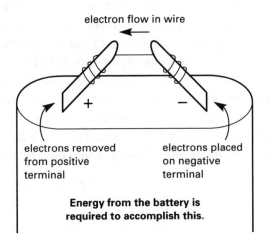

electron flow in wire

+

–

electrons removed from positive terminal

electrons placed on negative terminal

Energy from the battery is required to accomplish this.

The battery is the supply of energy, which comes out as heat in the wire. You could think of the battery as an electron pump.

Unfortunately, electrons were not known about when the idea of currents were first investigated. It was decided that, by convention, conventional current would flow from positive to negative in the wire. This was all right because the flow of charge could not be observed directly. But now we know that electrons do the flowing and that they flow in the opposite direction!

Electrons always flow in the opposite direction to conventional current. This means that **electrons flow from negative to positive** whereas **conventional current is said to flow from positive to negative.** This often leads to confusion until you get used to it. Of course, batteries are not the only source of electrical potential energy or potential difference, and heating is not the only effect of an electric current. You only have to think about the electrical appliances you have in the home to realize that the effects of a current are many and diverse. Closely related to the heating effect is the lighting effect. In a filament light bulb, a metal filament is heated so strongly that it glows white hot. Gas discharge tubes give rise to fluorescent lighting. Here an electric current is passed through a low-pressure gas. This time when moving electrons collide with gas ions, energy in the form of light is emitted.

As we shall see later on, whenever there is an electric current there is *always* an associated **magnetic field** produced. (A magnetic force field is an area where a magnetic force field is felt in a similar way to the electric force field.) This magnetic field is used in the workings of an electric motor. The electric motor transfers electrical potential energy into kinetic energy.

Electric currents can also pass through certain liquids. Metals can be liquids under certain conditions, and mercury is liquid at room temperature. You may be surprised to know that non-metal liquids such as a salt solution will also allow an electric current to flow.

As we saw in Chapter 3, common salt is chemically known as sodium chloride. However, what is important here is that, when salt is dissolved in water, the positively charged sodium ions and the negatively charged chlorine ions are free to move around the liquid independently. If a pair of electrodes is immersed in the solution and if one (the **anode**) is made positive and the other (the **cathode**) is made negative, the positive sodium ions will drift towards the cathode, and the negative chlorine ions will drift towards the anode. This drift of charged particles constitutes an electric current. Chemical reactions take place at each of the electrodes, so we can say that electric currents can have a chemical effect.

Resistance

We have discussed the idea of electric currents as a flow of electrons through metals. We have seen how the presence of metal atoms (more strictly, ions) causes the electron flow to be constantly interrupted. This ability to resist the electron flow, and hence current, is called the **electrical resistance** of the wire. A resistance wire will cause the electrical energy supplied to be transferred to heat. A filament in a light bulb is really a piece of resistance wire.

In order to cause an electric current to flow, a potential difference needs to be applied. According to **Ohm's law**, the higher the resistance of the wire, the larger is the potential difference needed to cause the same current to flow. **Resistors** (devices designed to have a known resistance) are very important in the study of electricity. The most important points are as follows:

☐ **To get a current to flow through a resistor, a potential difference must be applied.**

☐ **It therefore follows that, if there is a current flowing through a resistor, there must be a difference in potential across its ends.**

☐ **For a given resistor, the larger the potential difference applied, the larger will be the current which flows.**

Remember, the source of electrical potential difference supplies energy to circuits. Resistors transfer electrical energy into heat and therefore dissipate electrical energy or remove energy from circuits. Because energy can be neither created or destroyed, the total energy supplied to a circuit by the batteries, for example, must be balanced by the energy dissipated by the components like resistors. Devices like motors also transfer energy out of the circuit. Mains-driven power supplies can be used in place of batteries to provide energy sources.

Circuits

Much of the work associated with electricity deals with circuits. As we have already seen, it is necessary to have a potential difference and a complete circuit for a current to flow. In terms of circuits, the idea of potential difference is not quite right. Potential difference exists between two points, whereas in circuits the electric charge flows in a loop. In other words, it ends up at the same place that it started from. In the process of flowing round the circuit, energy transfers have taken place.

Scientists use the term **EMF** to describe **the amount of energy needed to cause 1 coulomb of charge to carry out one complete circuit.** (Actually this is potentially confusing because the letters EMF stand for electro-motive force. In fact, force has nothing to do with it. Many of these terms were invented in the early days of electricity. We now have a deeper understanding of what we are talking about.) The role of the battery in a simple circuit is to provide this energy. In terms of circuits, then, the battery is said to have an EMF of so many volts. This is the same thing as the potential difference between its terminals when there is no current flowing through it.

Take a look at this drawing of a simple circuit. It shows a battery connected to a light bulb in a holder with wires. Also shown is a piece of board with two drawing pins and a paper clip, arranged in such a way that when the paper-clip is held down, it forms a bridge between the two drawing pins and connects the two wires.

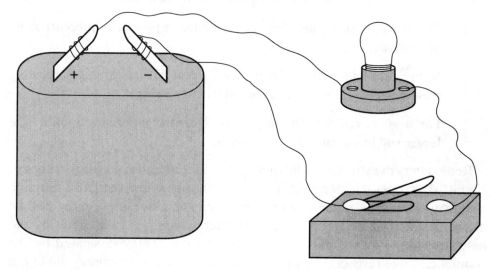

This drawing could be used to communicate a method of forming a circuit. There are several drawbacks. One is that it is not an easy drawing to accomplish. Second, it would become too complicated to follow very quickly as more components were added. Third, it applies only to the specific components illustrated. The same effect could be produced by using a different type of battery. It would make no difference to the overall working of the circuit.

It is for this reason that scientists and engineers have developed a schematic form of circuit diagram with agreed conventions for the representation of components. Compare the previous drawing with the circuit diagram on page 105. Notice how much easier it is to draw. Notice also how universal it is in application. It does not matter which type of battery, switch or light bulb you choose, the diagram is still usable. It is worth getting to know these symbols as they will come up again and again in work on electricity.

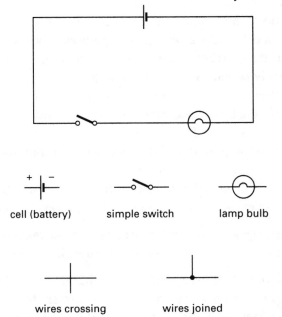

cell (battery)   simple switch   lamp bulb

wires crossing   wires joined

What is the switch for? It is used to turn the current on and off, of course, but how does it work? To answer this question, you need to think about what is required for a current to flow. A complete circuit is required. If the circuit is broken in some way, the current will cease. A simple switch is a controlled way of breaking the circuit. The domestic light switches in your house work on exactly this principle.

Now consider the light bulb. A light bulb is a device that is used to transfer electrical energy into light energy. How is this achieved? Recall that one of the effects of an electric current is to produce heating. The filament of the light bulb is made of resistance wire, which as we have seen will cause the electrical energy supplied to be transferred into heat. It is made so hot that it glows.

Think about the source of this energy. The cell or battery provides a source of electrical potential energy. This causes the electrons in the circuit to flow or gain kinetic energy. As the charges pass through the light bulb filament, this kinetic energy is transferred into heat energy. This means that the charges' potential energy has been transferred to kinetic energy, which has in turn been transferred to heat energy of the filament. The charged electrons that emerge from the light bulb having flowed through have less potential energy than they had as they entered. There is therefore a potential difference across the light bulb.

The battery is a source of electrical potential energy (EMF), but the light bulb acts as a drain for this energy. The light bulb has a higher electrical resistance than the connecting wires. If we neglect the resistance of these wires (this is usually a safe bet) and any resistance that the battery may have inside it (not such a safe bet), the potential difference across the light bulb equals the EMF of the cell. In other words, **energy in equals energy out.** It is important to notice here that the current flows *through* the light bulb. The potential difference appears between its ends, or *across* it.

How much energy does the light bulb transfer out of the circuit? Remember that potential difference is concerned with the amount of energy needed to move 1 coulomb of charge. The amount of energy that the light bulb uses depends not only on the potential difference across it, but also on the amount of charge that flows through it. Remember also that the current is the rate of flow of this charge. We are left with the result that the amount of energy that the light bulb uses every second (this is called the **power**) is such that:

- **The greater the potential difference, the greater the power.**
- **The greater the electric current, the greater the power.**

How can this be controlled? Remember that the light bulb has resistance. A body with electrical resistance acts to reduce the current that is allowed to flow when a particular potential difference is applied. In fact, the greater this resistance is, the smaller the current becomes. As we have just seen, the smaller the current becomes, the less power is transferred.

Is it possible to use one battery to light up more than one light bulb? Yes, of course it is. One way of doing this is to arrange the light bulbs end to end as shown in the following circuit diagram.

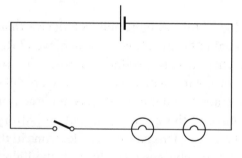

bulb A   bulb B

This way of connecting light bulbs is called a **series** arrangement. Now we need to think about how bright the light bulbs will be. Let us use the previous circuit diagram, where a single bulb is lit by a single battery, as a reference. This bulb will be referred to as being 'normally bright'.

How is it possible to predict how bright the bulbs will be in the new circuit? The brightness of the bulb is determined by how much electrical energy the bulb is converting to light energy every second. To start with, consider the potential difference across each bulb, and compare it with the potential difference across the single bulb in the earlier illustration of a simple circuit with a bulb and battery. In a simple circuit with a single bulb, the potential difference will be the same as the EMF of the cell. (In practice, it will be slightly less, but the difference will be ignored here and in all future analyses in this section.) Now think about the two bulbs in series. The battery is a source of electrical potential which supplies the energy necessary for electric charge to pass through the two bulbs. This potential energy is transferred to kinetic energy of the moving charges and then into heat and light energy in the light bulb. In order to find its way completely around the circuit, each coulomb of charge has to pass through each of the light bulbs in turn.

☐ **The total amount of energy available to each coulomb per complete circuit is the same whether you have one bulb or more in series.**

The charge is provided with a certain amount of energy by the battery. Each coulomb of charge has to pass through first one bulb and then the other. Potential energy is eventually transferred into heat and light energy by each bulb. Half the charge's potential energy is therefore transferred by the first bulb and the rest by the second.

Each coulomb of charge in the series circuit is able to contribute only half the amount of energy that was possible in the single bulb circuit. To find out how much energy is transferred in each bulb in each second, it is necessary to consider the rate at which the charge is flowing around the circuit. In other words, the next item to take into account is the current which is flowing.

Before analysing the current in the present circuit, it is useful here to think about electric current in a more general way. Many people fall into the trap of considering each coulomb of charge in isolation. This leads them to follow the progress of this isolated coulomb of charge around the circuit. The trap is that they might begin to think in terms of the coulomb passing first through one light bulb and then through the other. This can lead to the erroneous conclusion that it is possible to turn the switch on, allow the first bulb to light up and then turn off the switch before the charge has reached the second bulb. This would mean that the first bulb would flash on and off, but the second bulb would not have time to light up.

This way of thinking compares the circuit with watching a racing car driving around a race track. The car takes each bend in turn. It is possible to bring the car to a halt after only half a lap, by which time it will have negotiated some corners but not others. Only when the whole lap has been completed can we say that all the corners have been turned.

The reality of an electric circuit is more accurately represented by a fairground ride of the type where a number of cars are linked together front to back. No car is unconnected either at the front or at the back. The whole circuit is occupied by cars. When the ride begins *all the cars* start moving in unison. When the ride ends all the cars come to rest together. After any period of time, any part of the circuit will have had the same number of cars passing it as any other part. So it is with electric circuits. As soon as the circuit is completed by closing the switch, charge all around the circuit begins to move. Both bulbs will therefore light up and go out together.

Now let's return to the series circuit. Each light bulb behaves like a resistance. Remember that a resistance will cause the electrical energy supplied to be converted to heat. Recall also that **for a given resistor, the larger the potential difference applied, the larger will be the current that flows.**

This means that, since each light bulb has the same resistance and since each has only half the EMF of the cell applied to it, the current will be half the current that flows through the bulb in the earlier illustration of a simple circuit with a bulb and battery. So for each bulb the energy transferred per coulomb is halved and the number of coulombs per second (the current) is halved. It is safe to say that each bulb will be comparatively dim.

The analysis of the series circuit makes clear the vital importance of the potential difference across components and the electric current flowing through them. Because these quantities are so important, devices have been designed to measure them. A device to measure potential difference is called a **voltmeter** and a device to measure electric current is called an **ammeter.** Resistors are quite useful as well, so they are given their own symbol. Some resistors are adjustable (like the volume control on your TV set) and these have a special circuit symbol. Here are some more circuit symbols to add to your collection!

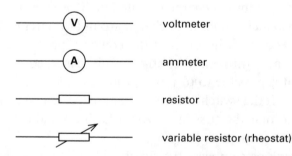

Think about *another* way of connecting two light bulbs to a battery so that they both light up. On the next page is a circuit diagram showing this second arrangement, where the light bulbs are said to be **in parallel.** Notice that ammeters and voltmeters have been placed at appropriate places.

Since electric currents flow *through* devices an ammeter must be placed in such a way that the current that it is to measure must flow through it. Ammeter A1, for example, will have the same current flowing through it as bulb 1, so it will register the current flowing through bulb 1. Can you think

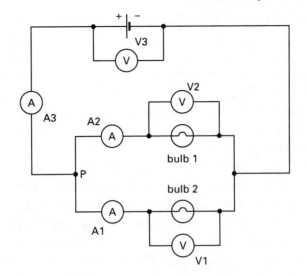

what device the ammeter A3 is measuring the current through? It is measuring the current through the battery, of course. You could also think of it as measuring the current through the pair of bulbs at once!

Potential differences appear between the terminals of devices (it is a measure of the difference of potential energy of the charge between one end of the component and the other). Voltmeters measure the potential difference between their terminals. They are therefore placed *across* devices. So voltmeter V1 will measure the potential difference *across* bulb 1.

At this point, there is something else you should know. **If two points in a circuit are connected directly by a wire of negligible resistance, they are at virtually the same potential.**

This means that there is no potential difference between places connected by wires. Look carefully at the circuit diagram. Trace the wire from the negative terminal of V1 towards V2. Repeat this for V3. You should find that the three negative terminals are connected together. This means that they are at the same potential.

An ideal ammeter has zero resistance. It may be treated as if it were just a piece of wire. Now assure yourself that the positive terminals of the three voltmeters are connected and that they also are at the same potential. What does this tell you about the readings on the three voltmeters?

Of course, each of the voltmeters will give the same reading. This means that it is not necessary to employ all three meters. One would suffice. Where would you place this one meter? It does not matter which of the three places you choose – each is as good as any other, provided the ammeters act as wires in this regard.

Next let's consider the brightness of the bulbs. Each bulb has the same potential difference across it as the EMF of the cell. As we have seen, for a given resistor (and the light bulb can be considered as a resistor remember) the current that flows depends upon the potential difference applied. So each of the light bulbs must glow normally bright. This might seem odd at first because one battery is being used to light more than one bulb. The limiting factor is what current the battery can deliver. There is a limit to how many bulbs a given battery can drive like this. How does this affect how long the battery can last before it goes 'flat'?

Think about what is happening to the currents as measured by the ammeters. A1 and A2 measure the current through each of the bulbs. This is the normal current for the bulb. What do you expect ammeter A3 will show? Current is flow of charge. The current which flows through A3 splits two ways when it reaches the branch to the light bulb at point P. Since each bulb is the same, each will take the same current. This means that the current passing through A3 is double that passing through each of A1 and A2. The battery therefore supplies energy at twice the rate it would if it were lighting only one bulb. It will therefore last only half as long as with two bulbs.

It is easy to see how useful light bulbs are. They provide a source of light from electrical energy. What about a simple resistor? What can it be used for? Think about the series light bulb circuit. The presence of the second light bulb reduces the brightness of the other. The current which flows is less than it would have been if only one bulb had been present. A resistor will have the same effect as a light bulb. It serves to reduce the current flowing. If a *variable* resistor is used in place of one of the light bulbs, it can be used to regulate or control the brightness of the remaining bulb. If an electric motor is used in place of the light bulb, the variable resistor can be used to regulate the speed at which the motor turns. As was mentioned earlier, such a device can be used to control the sound level coming from your television set, or even to control the brightness or colour. Variable resistors are very useful in this sort of way.

MAGNETISM

The majority of people are introduced to the subject of magnetism by looking at **permanent magnets.** These are the horseshoe or bar magnets commonly found in toy shops and school science kits. In many ways it is a shame that this is how magnetism is first encountered. It gives the impression that magnetism is associated with permanent magnets and that you can mimic these magnets with electrical trickery to form electromagnets. In reality, magnetism is properly associated with electric current, and it is the bar magnets which are the oddity! However, because of this common experience with permanent magnets, it is with these that we will start.

Most people know that magnets are able to attract each other and are able to attract or 'pick up' certain 'magnetic' materials such as steel pins and paper-clips. This shows that there is an attractive force at the heart of magnetism. Not so many people are aware of the repulsive force that is also associated with magnetism.

A typical bar magnet will have two ends which are often coloured differently. Most commonly they are coloured red and blue. If the red end of one magnet is held near the blue end of another, a force of attraction between them will be felt. If, however, two blue ends are held together, or two red ends for that matter, the force between the magnets becomes repulsive. This force is really only noticeable with strong magnets. If you want to experience this yourself, you could use 'ceramic' magnets. Alternatively, you can see the repulsive forces at work if you float a pair of bar magnets on little wooden rafts on the surface of still water.

The two ends of the magnet are called **poles. The basic law of magnetism is that like poles repel and unlike poles attract.**

The Earth has its own 'permanent' magnetism due to its iron core. One of the *magnetic* poles is close to the Earth's *geographic* North Pole and the other is close to the Earth's *geographic* South Pole. If left to move freely like a compass needle, magnets will automatically line up in this north–south orientation. For this reason the poles are labelled north and south. North magnetic poles will point towards (are attracted to) geographic north, whereas south magnetic poles will point south. This must mean that the magnetic pole at the Earth's North Pole is in fact a magnetic south! Think about it.

The fact that magnetic forces can be felt near a bar magnet means that once again, as in the case of electricity, we talk about **force fields.** By now you will be becoming familiar with the idea of a force field. We have met gravitational force fields, which surround all bodies with mass. The gravitational force between bodies results from an interaction between their gravitation fields. We have met electrical force fields, which surround all bodies with charge. The electrical force between charged bodies results from an interaction between these electrical force fields. Now we come to magnetic force fields, which surround moving bodies that carry electric charges. The forces between such bodies result from an interaction between the magnetic force fields.

The source of the moving charges may not be immediately obvious. In the case of permanent magnets, the moving charges concerned are the electrons surrounding the nuclei of the iron atoms. Actually, nuclei themselves carry charge and also spin, so it is possible to have magnetic fields associated with the nucleus! Hydrogen nuclei have the largest 'nuclear' magnetic field. Doctors make use of this with the new nuclear magnetic resonance imaging devices, which they use for a similar purpose to X-rays.

Just like electric force fields, magnetic fields are represented by drawing lines with arrows on. These **field lines** have some strange properties. They behave like tightly bundled strands of stretched elastic, in that they are always trying to become shorter. Also the individual strands seem to push each other away. This is what is meant by the **interaction** between the magnetic fields.

Let's look at the force between two permanent magnets.

The direction of the arrow is the direction of the force that would be felt by a free north pole placed at that point. It should be pointed out here that it is not possible to have a single magnetic pole. If you cut a bar magnet in half, you do

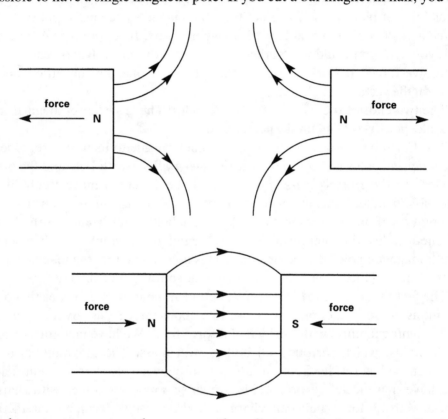

not have two separate poles, one north and one south, but two smaller bar magnets.

To 'see' a magnetic field all you have to do is sprinkle iron filings on to a sheet of paper placed over a bar magnet and tap the paper gently. Alternatively, you can plot a magnetic field line by using a tiny plotting compass. To do this, place the magnet on a plain sheet of paper and put the compass near one end. Mark the paper where the needle of the compass points to. Replace the compass so that the end which originally pointed to the magnet now sits over the mark on the paper, and repeat the process. When you have finished, join up the dots to produce a magnetic field line.

Electricity and magnetism

In 1819 the Professor of Physics at Copenhagen, Hans Christian Oersted, discovered that whenever there is an electric current flowing there is always an associated magnetic field. This field takes the form of concentric circles around the wire carrying the current. The diagram below illustrates this field. Note the direction of the arrows.

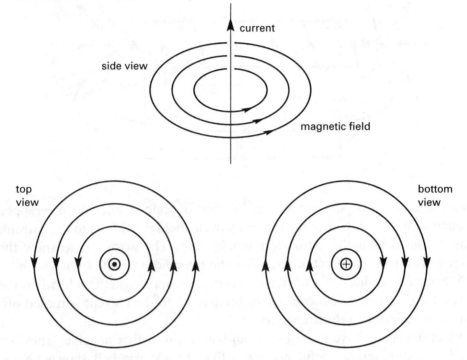

In order to remember the directions of the field lines, try the following. Use your right hand to give a thumbs-up gesture. If your thumb represents the direction of the electric current then your fingers will represent the direction of the magnetic field. You are urged to try this!

The magnetic field strength depends upon several things. First, it depends upon the size of the current. The larger the current, the larger the field strength. Also important are the length of the wire, the distance from the wire and the nature of the material in the space around the wire.

If you want to make the field stronger, you can accomplish this by increasing the current. This works up to a point, but it does present problems of overheating the wires themselves. Remember, electric currents produce heating effects. A clever way around this is to wrap the wire round and round in a circle to produce a coil. For example, if the wire is wrapped round a pencil and all along its length, a particular type of coil called a **solenoid** is produced. The more turns of wire you have on your pencil, the stronger will be the field produced. If you replace the pencil with an iron nail, the field becomes even stronger still.

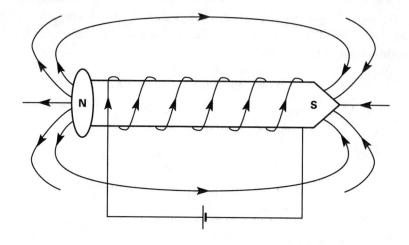

The diagram above shows the field produced when a solenoid is wrapped around an iron nail. Notice the direction of the field in relation to the current. The N and S with the arrows on should help. The arrows here show the direction of the current in the wire when the solenoid is viewed from one end.

What we have here is a device which produces a magnetic field when the current flows, and which loses its magnetism when the current is turned off. We have designed an **electromagnet.**

Electromagnets have more uses than you might at first imagine. They are used in a number of useful devices – like the electric bell shown on the opposite page. The bell makes use of what is called the 'make and break' circuit.

The diagram on page 115 shows how the bell works. When switch D is open, the spring holds the contacts A and B together. The clapper C is far from the gong G. When the circuit is completed by closing the switch, a current flows. This causes the solenoid to act as a magnet and to attract the iron pole piece E of the bell armature. As it moves towards the magnet, the armature causes the clapper to strike the bell. The movement also causes the contacts at A and B to become separated and the circuit is broken. The current ceases to flow and the magnet ceases to attract E. The springiness returns the armature to its original position. Contacts A and B are joined once again and the whole process is repeated.

Motors

There is another, perhaps even more widely used, application of electro-

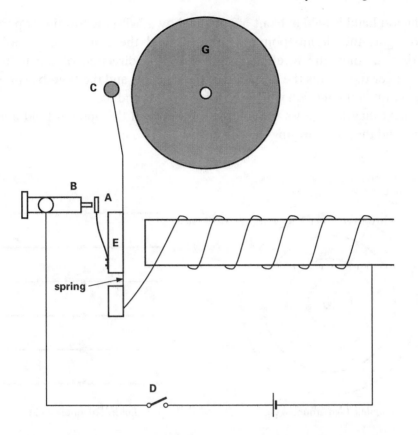

magnetism. It is concerned with the so-called **motor-rule.** It so happens that if a wire carrying an electric current is placed in and at right angles to a magnetic field, it will experience a force at right angles to both the field and the direction of the current. The reason for this is that the field produced by the current in the wire interacts with the applied field to result in a magnetic force. It can be difficult to work out the direction of this force, so here is an easy way of remembering the directions. It is called **Fleming's left-hand rule.** It is not really a rule at all, merely a mnemonic.

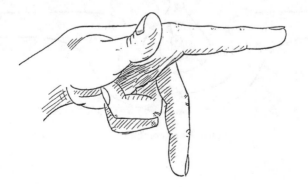

If the left hand is held in front of you, as shown, with the forefinger pointing left to right, the thumb pointing upwards and the centre finger pointing towards you, then the forefinger represents the direction of the **field**, the centre finger represents the direction of the **current**, and the thumb represents the direction of the **motion** which the force would produce.

The next diagram shows the interaction between the applied field and the field around the wire carrying the current.

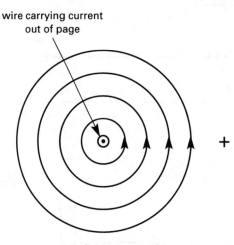

magnetic field around a wire

+

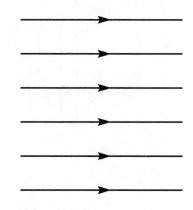

uniform magnetic field

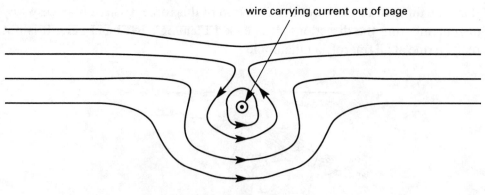

the two fields combined

If a coil of wire is placed in a magnetic field between two magnets, a rotating electric motor can be produced.

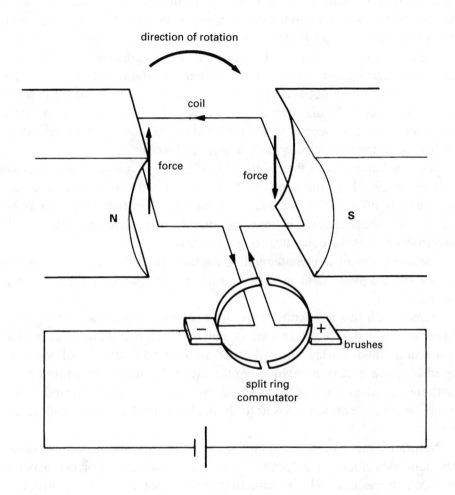

The above diagram shows a simple DC electric motor. Notice that the force on one side of the coil is up, while the force on the other side is down. This pair of forces produces a twisting effect which will cause the coil to rotate. Notice also the so-called split ring commutator. If it were not for the commutator, it would not be possible for the coil to execute more than one half-turn. When the right hand side of the coil reaches its lowest position, it needs to have the current in it reversed so that it can experience an upward force to keep it rotating. The ring to which it is attached breaks contact with the positive brush and makes contact with the negative one. The other arm of the coil behaves in opposite but corresponding fashion.

Electromagnetic induction

Michael Faraday, of the Royal Institution in London, was extremely interested in the study of electricity and magnetism. In the nineteenth century he discovered that if a coil is placed in series with a sensitive **galvanometer** (a kind of ammeter used to detect current rather than to measure it) so as to make a complete circuit, and then a magnet is plunged into the coil, the galvanometer registers a current. If the magnet is held stationary, even inside the coil, no reading appears. He also noticed that if the magnet is removed, the galvanometer again registers a current, but this time in the opposite direction. It is not necessary for the magnet to move – the effect is just as noticeable if the magnet stays still and the coil moves.

We now know that, if the magnetic field in the vicinity of a wire is caused to change, an EMF (remember, an EMF is provided by a battery to drive a current around a circuit) is *induced* in the wire. The field change may be due to moving magnets, or it may be due to the changing strength of an electromagnet as the current through it changes.

Faraday's law of electromagnetic induction states that the faster the rate at which the magnetic field associated with a wire changes, the greater is the induced EMF.

Armed with this new knowledge, let's review the electric motor. After all, here we have a device where a whole coil of wire is caused to rotate when near a magnetic field. Surely this will cause an induced EMF. This EMF could be used to drive a current, which would cause the motor to continue to turn without the need for a battery. Once the motor has been started it will run itself, won't it? You are advised to think about this for a while before moving on.

Naturally, there must be a flaw in the above argument because motors of the kind described do not exist! In part the analysis is correct. An EMF *is* induced in the coil. The reason that it does not allow the motor to work without a battery is because it does not act in the same direction as the battery. It works in the opposite direction and is therefore called a **back-EMF.**

This has to be the case if you think about it, otherwise you would have a motor which produces kinetic energy and electrical energy at the same time. This goes against the conservation of energy principle. (Remember, energy cannot be created or destroyed.)

The idea of a back-EMF was discovered by Henry Lenz, a nineteenth-century Russian physicist.

Lenz's law of electromagnetism induction states that the direction of the induced EMF is always such as to try to oppose the change that is causing it.

Think about a circuit with a motor and a battery and nothing else. The battery supplies an EMF, which provides the potential energy necessary for the current to flow. The motor transfers this potential energy to kinetic energy. In terms of the circuit, it removes potential energy in the same way as the resistor removed it to transfer it to heat. The potential difference across the resistor was in the opposite direction to the EMF of the cell, so the potential difference across the motor, or back-EMF, also acts in opposition to the battery.

Generating electricity

The idea of a motor that generates its own electrical energy is not a complete waste of time though. If an *external* source of kinetic energy is used to turn the coil in the magnetic field, an EMF will be induced which can be used to drive a current. What we have here is a device that is able to transfer kinetic energy into electrical energy. The commercial electricity-generating companies often use turbines driven by steam to drive the generators.

The diagram below shows a simplified version of a dynamo or electricity generator. The design is basically similar to the DC motor except that there is

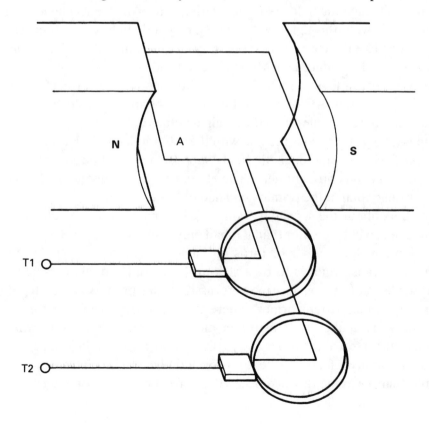

no battery, only two terminals to use as outlets. Also there are two complete rings instead of one split ring.

How can you predict which way the EMF will be induced? There are two ways to do this. One way is to use the motor rule to see which way the EMF would have to be in order to drive the coil in the given direction. Then, because of Lenz's law, the induced EMF will be in the opposite direction. The other way is to notice that, if you try using your right hand instead of your left hand in the motor rule position, with the forefinger and thumb pointing in the same direction as before, your centre finger will be pointing in the opposite direction to what it was before. If you like, then, you can use the left-hand rule for motors and the right-hand rule for dynamos. Frankly, this second method can get mixed up, so it is recommended you use the former.

Notice that, as side A of the coil is moving up, terminal T1 will be positive; when it reaches the other side and starts moving down, T1 will become negative. Such a generator will produce AC electricity.

Transformers

As we have already concluded, moving coils or magnets are not the only ways to change the magnetic field associated with a wire. An electromagnet with an AC current flowing through it will create a magnetic field which is constantly changing just like the current, first one way and then the other. This changing field can be used to induce an EMF in a second coil.

This is the principle upon which the transformer works. A transformer is a device for converting AC of one voltage to AC of another voltage. This may be either greater or smaller than the original voltage.

Suppose the primary coil, the one with the AC applied to it, has many turns. It will produce a strong magnetic field. Suppose a second (secondary, would you believe?) coil is brought near. The effect that the magnetic field has on it will be stronger than if the primary coil had only a few turns.

Now think about the secondary coil. If it has many turns, the effect of the magnetic field will be greater than if it had only a few turns.

By choosing the number of turns on each coil carefully, you can decide whether the transformer is to be a **step-up** (increasing voltage) transformer, where the secondary coil has more turns than the primary, or a **step-down** (decreasing voltage) transformer, where the secondary has fewer turns than the primary. To make the transformer more efficient, it is usual to wind the two coils one on top of the other and to place an iron core at the centre.

It is the ability of AC to be transformed that makes it so much more versatile than DC electric currents. AC electricity is used for electric power distribution systems, where high voltages are used for transmission and then transformed into lower voltages for domestic use.

DOMESTIC ELECTRICITY

Electricity is produced in power stations, of course. These are placed all over the country, depending on many factors. Nuclear power stations, for example, are often placed on the coast – and certainly far from centres of population wherever possible. Hydroelectric power stations are placed wherever the geographical conditions are right. In many cases, the centres of electricity generation are far from the ultimate consumers.

In many countries, the power stations are all connected together to form a giant **grid** or network of cables for electricity distribution. This is a useful arrangement because some types of power station can quickly and easily have their output modified, so that the distribution companies can match the supply to the demand. Other types of power station are slow to react. These can be kept constantly on line to supply the basic minimum power that the grid is likely to service.

One difficulty which has to be overcome in the supply and distribution of electricity is the power loss suffered as the electricity passes through the transmission cables. These cables are made to have the smallest resistance possible by constructing them of highly conducting materials, such as copper, and as thick as practicable. The problem is that cable is expensive, and the thicker it is, the more expensive it becomes.

Any cable has to have a resistance. The longer the cable is, the higher is its overall resistance. Many distribution cables are tens and even hundreds of kilometres long. In common with any resistor, the heating effect of the electricity depends upon the size of the electric current that flows. To reduce the energy losses due to heating, it is necessary to keep the size of the current as small as possible. On the other hand, the whole purpose of the cable is to transmit electrical power! The power transmitted depends upon two factors: the current and the voltage. You can see that, if the current is reduced to save wastage, the voltage must be correspondingly increased to ensure sufficient power transmission. In the UK voltages up to 400,000 volts are used. Naturally, this kind of voltage would be most inappropriate for the domestic consumer!

Near centres of population, electricity substations (transformers) exist to reduce this voltage considerably. The actual voltages used vary from country to country. Nearer to the actual domestic outlets, the voltage is transformed again down to a much safer level. So you do not need to worry – you will not have 400,000 volts delivered to your kitchen!

Costing electricity

If you look carefully at any domestic electrical appliance, you will find a label attached to it explaining the correct voltage to use, the correct frequency of the AC supply and also the power that the device consumes. The power is measured in **watts** or **kilowatts.** A kilowatt is a thousand watts.

Your electricity bill is calculated from the amount of electrical energy that you have used (transferred). The unit that the suppliers of electricity use is based on the power that the appliance consumes and the length of time for which it is operated. Obviously, the higher the power of the device, the more electricity it will consume in a given time. Also the longer that the device is using the electricity, the more energy it will transfer. The unit used by the electricity industry is the **kilowatt-hour.**

Electrical safety

Electricity is dangerous . . . it can kill! Most domestic fires in the western world are caused by electrical problems. Domestic electricity supplies are of sufficiently high voltage to electrocute you.

We have already seen that, in order for an electric current to flow, a complete circuit is necessary. If you touch a live wire, you will get a shock only if a current passes through your body. This will happen only if a complete circuit is made. In most cases the Earth – that is, planet Earth – forms a path for the electric current to find its way back to the transformer supplying your property. If you have one hand touching a live wire and you are in contact with (standing on) the Earth, you will be part of a complete circuit!

Electrical appliances are designed in such a way as to minimize this risk. Live wires should not be exposed. If a fault develops with a live wire – perhaps it becomes dislodged through misuse – it may make contact with the outer parts of the appliance. Some appliances avoid this eventuality by being **double insulated.** This means that there are two layers of insulating material between the live connection and the outside world. Both layers would need to be breached for the appliance to become live on the outside.

There is another strategy, however. In many appliances a wire which is connected electrically to the Earth is attached to the outer parts. This wire is called the **earth wire.** The convention in Europe is that such wires are green and yellow candy-striped. If the live wire should come into contact with the outer parts of the appliance, the current will find its way to Earth through the earth wire in preference to the body of any person who touches it. The current will flow through the wire because it has far less resistance than the human body.

This tendency for current to take the path of least resistance is the cause of another potential hazard. In normal circumstances, the current will pass through a motor or the filament of a light bulb or some other components that will drain the energy from the circuit. But if the live wire becomes dislodged, it may come into contact with the normal return path for the circuit. In this case the current will pass directly from the live wire to the return wire. It will by-pass the energy-using component in what is called a **short circuit.** The low resistance of the new circuit means that the current which flows will increase considerably, beyond the capacity of the cables to carry it without burning out. To prevent this, devices called **fuses** are placed in the circuit. These are set to melt and thus interrupt the flow of current if it should exceed a predetermined value. The fuse is placed near the point where the live wire enters the system.

In more recent times, devices called **residual current circuit breakers** (RCCBs, or sometimes RCDs, which stands for residual current devices) are fitted. These are able to detect tiny differences between the current in the live supply wire and the current in the neutral return wire. If such a difference exists, they break the circuit. Thus, if some current is entering the system but not leaving it properly, it must be leaking to Earth somewhere and this is a fault. It is quite common to use RCCBs with outdoor appliances like electric lawn-mowers.

As a final warning, **if you see someone who is experiencing an electric shock, do not touch them**, even to try to pull them away. *You* will receive a shock as well as them. Rather, you should **isolate the supply** by unplugging the device or turning it off at the mains. Only when the current has been turned off is it safe to approach the patient.

Chapter 5

Waves

INTRODUCTION

Let's start off by looking at this series of apparently unconnected events:

- A distant bell is struck and you hear the ringing sound.
- You are out at sea. A lighthouse on a nearby headland flashes.
- You hurl a stone into a lake. After a short while the ripples formed lap at the pool's edge near your feet.
- A tight string is wiggled at one end and the disturbance travels along the string.

Each of these occurrences seems different from the others, yet they all have something in common. In each case the event is initiated at a point in time and space – the bell is struck, the light flashes, the stone lands in the water . . . The disturbance travels through space so that its effects are felt some time later at some distant point. Scientists would say that each of these events results in an example of **wave motion.**

You may be tempted to ask the question, 'What exactly is a wave?' It is the intention here to study examples of wave motion and attempt to understand the properties of waves. In this way, you will become familiar with the concept of waves better than if some science textbook-style description is offered.

Let's begin by looking at the ripple on the surface of the water in the lake. Before we begin, a word of caution. We are interested here in the ripples as they appear in the middle of the lake. They might just as well be waves in the middle of the ocean. The waves that you see crashing on the sea-shore have been affected by the presence of the beach itself and are therefore *not* useful for a first analysis of wave motion. For this reason, then, we will concentrate on waves in the middle of the lake or ocean.

Think very carefully about what is going on here. What is happening is that a disturbance on the surface of the water is moving out from where the stone landed. To make things simpler, we will begin by concentrating only on the motion of this disturbance in a line radiating out from the centre of disturbance.

Now imagine there is a buoy floating out on the lake. This buoy is caused to bob up and down in some way, perhaps by a diver deep under the surface pulling on a rope attached to the bottom of the buoy. The buoy moves up and down in a regular way. If you watch it for a period of time, you will notice that it moves down to a minimum depth, then up to a maximum height, from where it returns to its starting point. The whole process is then repeated over and over. The buoy can be said to be **oscillating.** Every time it reaches its starting point and is moving downwards (remember that it passes through its starting point on its way from its lowest point to its highest point as well as on its way back down again), it completes another oscillation.

Let's assume that the diver keeps the motion of the buoy uniform. It will then take the same amount of time to execute each oscillation. This time ought to be of some significance. Let's call it the **period of oscillation** – the time taken for the buoy to undergo **one complete oscillation.**

There is another way of looking at the variation in the position of this buoy as time goes on. Instead of measuring the time it takes the buoy to oscillate once, we might try counting the number of oscillations it is forced to undergo in a given period of time. It would make sense to use one second as the amount of time used. We now have a measure of the number of oscillations that happen every second. This is also given a special name. It is called the **frequency.**

Imagine now that you place a cork in the water a short distance away from the buoy. What do you think its motion will be like? You need to be careful here. You might be misled into thinking that the cork would be propelled by the wave and travel across the surface of the water. A quick play with floating objects in the bath should soon convince you that this is not the case, although it *is* a commonly held misconception. You see it is *the ripple* that moves across the water. There is no lump of water moving across the surface. So the cork does not move across the water, but has a very similar motion to the buoy itself. It also bobs up and down.

It is not easy to grasp this difference between the up and down motion of the water and the outward motion of the ripple or wave. Sometimes when you look into the sea, the surface is not as clean as we would wish it to be. All sorts of debris sometimes floats on the surface. If you look at the water and observe waves passing, you will be able to see the wave moving across the surface while the debris moves up and down. The pattern of rubbish on the surface can still be recognized, despite the disturbance caused by the passing wave. You really need to be happy about this idea before you continue.

It is not just water waves that behave in this way. Think about the wave that travels along a stretched string. Imagine that you have dabbed a drop of bright paint on a small section of a piece of string. Think what you would see if you watched the motion of just this painted section as you waggled one end and a wave moved along the string. You would see the painted part move up and down. Such waves, where the motion of the wave is at right angles to the direction of the disturbance, are called **transverse waves.**

Let's go back to the water waves. So far we have been considering the way that the surface of the water at a particular point along the wave behaves as time passes. Now think about the way the surface changes with distance from the buoy at a given point in time.

Think about how a photograph of the water would appear. A photograph would give us an image of the water surface captured at an instant (well, modern cameras have really fast shutter speeds, so it is nearly an instant) in time. Remember, we are not looking down at the circular patterns of the waves, but rather at a cut-through view of how the surface appearance changes as you move out from the centre of the disturbance. You may well observe a pattern like the one shown here.

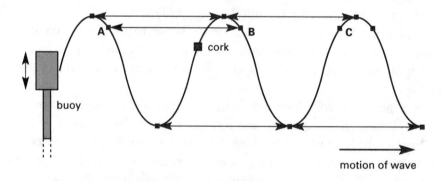

The distance between any two *corresponding* points on a pair of adjacent waves is always the same. The peaks are the same distance apart, the troughs are the same distance apart and so are any other corresponding points like A and B. C may be at the same level as A and B, but it does not correspond. Can you see why? This distance between corresponding points is given a special name. It is called the **wavelength.**

Now let's go back to the cork. You will notice that it happens to be in a corresponding position to the buoy. Think about the behaviour of the buoy and the cork as time passes. Sure enough, they both bob up and down, they both oscillate. Naturally, the frequency of each is the same. There is a bit more to it than that though. Look again at the points representing the peaks. They have all reached the highest point together. That is what it means to be corresponding points. The fact is that, in common with all corresponding points, the cork and the buoy move up and down in step with one another. We say that they are **in phase** with one another. This only happens because in our example the buoy and the cork are at corresponding points. If the cork were at point A instead, the two could oscillate with the same frequency but would be out of step – they would be **out of phase.**

Look now at a point which is at a peak. Compare it with another point at a trough. When the first point is at its peak, the second is at the trough position. These two points are separated by exactly one-half of a wavelength. They oscillate with the same frequency, but their directions of motion are always opposite. We say that they are in **antiphase.**

Think about how the water would appear without waves. It would be flat and still. A section cut through it would look like a horizontal straight line. The water has not been disturbed by any wave. We could call this line **the line of zero displacement.** It is the equilibrium position for the water. Look now at this diagram, which shows two views at once. One is a section through undisturbed water. The other is *the same water* with waves passing through.

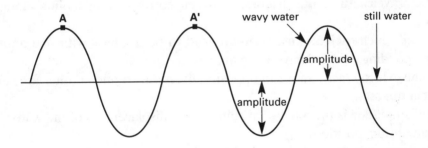

Notice that the displacement of the surface of the water varies from place to place. (It will also vary from time to time, of course.) At the time when the image was 'frozen', points A and A' were at the peak. Their displacement was at its maximum. The distance between the peak and the equilibrium line is also given a special name. It is called the **amplitude.**

The amplitude of the wave gives us an indication of the size of the disturbance. Notice that the amplitude is measured from the equilibrium position to the peak (or from the equilibrium position to the trough) and *not from peak to trough.*

If you were to sit on the bank of the lake and watch the water, what would you see? You would see a series of waves emanating from the buoy and moving away from it. We have analysed the movement of the water and have decided that it moves up and down only. Yet you still are left with the impression of something moving along the surface of the water. What moves is the **disturbance.** You can see the peaks and troughs travelling across the water.

We can, in some ways, treat the pattern of the wave as if it were a real object, and talk about the wave moving over the water. Things which move have a velocity, and what we are talking about here is the **wave velocity.** (The velocity of the wave is constant: that is, the wave moves at a steady speed. Do not confuse this with the up and down motion of the water, which varies from place to place and from time to time. Remember, the cork moves upwards, then stops, and then moves downwards.)

Summary of terms used so far

You have been introduced to a number of new terms. Let's pause for a while and re-examine these.

The **period of oscillation** is the time taken for the cork or the buoy or any part of the water to undergo one complete cycle.

The **frequency** is the number of complete oscillations undergone in one second.

The **wavelength** is the distance between corresponding points along the wave.

Points which oscillate in unison are said to be **in phase** with one another. Corresponding points always move in phase.

Points which *always* move in opposite directions to one another are said to be in **antiphase.**

The **amplitude** is the maximum value of the displacement of the water from its equilibrium position.

The **wave velocity** is the speed with which the ripples appear to move over the surface of the water.

Types of waves

Waves where the disturbance appears to move in this way are called **travelling waves** or sometimes **progressive waves.**

Waves where the displacement is at right angles to the direction of motion of the wave are called **transverse waves.**

Not all waves are transverse. Have you ever played games with a slinky? A slinky is a metal strip wrapped up into a tight helix or spiral. Think about a slinky laid out on a long table, or a number of tables laid end to end. Imagine that one end of the slinky is held firm and the other end is stretched to the end of the table. Suppose the person holding this end suddenly executes a sharp backwards and forward motion with the hand holding the end of the slinky.

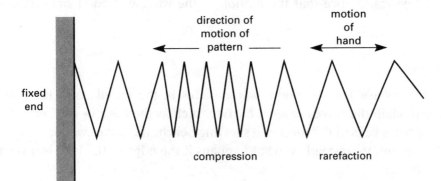

The slinky suddenly takes up the shape shown above. What is more, the closing-up of rings (**compression**) followed by the opening-up of rings (**rarefaction**) moves along the length of the slinky. Just for now we will ignore what happens when the disturbance meets the fixed end. What we have here is a disturbance travelling along the slinky. What we have here is a wave!

Waves where the disturbance is *parallel* to the direction of motion of the wave are called **longitudinal waves.** Imagine a queue of people holding hands. Think what would happen if you first pushed and then pulled the person at the front of the queue. The disturbance would travel along the queue as a longitudinal wave.

PROPERTIES OF WAVES

One of the reasons that scientists are interested in the study of waves is that there are so many different examples of wave motion in existence. If the properties of waves can be understood and if a new phenomenon can be established to be a wave, it can be expected that the new phenomenon will behave in a predictable way. So far we have really only examined water waves in detail, although we have also touched on other waves. The point is that what you have learned about water waves also applies to many other examples of waves. In addition, as they travel from one place to another, waves invariably carry energy with them. That property alone would merit a study of waves. So let's look at some of the properties common to all waves.

Before we begin it will be useful to discuss the idea of parallel waves. Let's think about disturbances in an ocean. Instead of considering circular wavefronts progressing outwards from a point of disturbance, like the bobbing buoy, we need to think about parallel troughs and crests moving across the surface driven by the wind. If you take an aerial photograph of this ocean at any time and draw a line to join up all the points that are at a crest at the time that the photograph was taken, then the line will be straight if you have truly parallel waves. Notice that the motion of the wave will be at right angles to this line.

Reflection

So far you have learned about water waves in the middle of a lake. What happens when the waves reach a barrier, such as the edge of the lake? If the edge of the lake is in the form of a shelving beach, the waves will be absorbed. Let's concentrate instead on what happens if the edge of the lake is a vertical concrete wall.

When the waves meet such a barrier, a strange thing happens. The waves seem to rebound. The following diagram shows how a photograph of a series of parallel waves will look as this rebounding process is taking place.

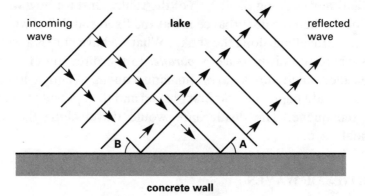

concrete wall

The diagram has included only a portion of the parallel wave for reasons of simplicity. The last three incoming and the first three outgoing waves are straightforward enough. It is the waves which are in the process of being reflected that need consideration. The part of the incoming wave closest to the wall meets it first and is therefore the first to rebound. Notice that the angles A and B marked on the diagram are equal.

The whole process is referred to as **reflection.** Reflection is a property of waves in general, and not just waves on water.

Diffraction

Suppose the parallel wave on the lake approaches a barrier such as a concrete pier. How will the surface of the water appear on the other side of the pier? You might expect it to appear as shown in the left half of the following diagram. In fact it would appear more like the right half.

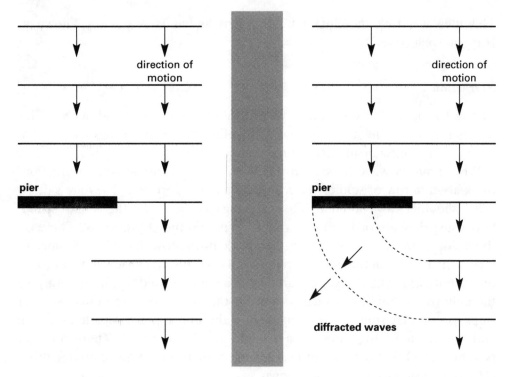

The appearance of waves behind the pier may at first surprise you. The phenomenon is known as **diffraction.** Scientists explain this by saying that each point on the wavefront of a parallel wave behaves as if it were itself a source of circular secondary wavelets. When there are lots of such points side by side, as in the case of a full parallel wave, the sideways waves produced by the one wavelet are cancelled out by those produced by its neighbour. The result is a new parallel wave. When the neighbour is removed – by an obstacle like a pier, for example – the wavelet on the edge is free to carry on without interference.

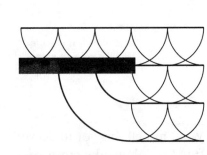

diffraction and wavelets

This idea was first thought of by Huygens and is consequently known as **Huygens' principle.**

Refraction

The last property of waves that we will discuss for now is refraction. This means *the change in direction* that a travelling wave undergoes as it moves from one transmission material or **medium** to another.

Why should a wave behave in this way? To try to understand refraction, think about a row of soldiers marching on a parade ground. They are side by side, shoulder to shoulder, all marching forwards at the same speed. Supposing they are ordered to turn left. What do they have to do? Those on the inside of the curve, on the left-hand side of the row, have less distance to march than those on the outside, right-hand side. It is not practicable for those on the outside to run (they are marching in a dignified and regular fashion), so the only way to make the turn is to order the inside soldiers to take smaller steps so that they slow down. Imagine now that they have completed the turn and are required to march in a straight line once again. There are two possibilities. One is for the slower soldiers on the inside to speed up; the other is for the outside soldiers to slow down.

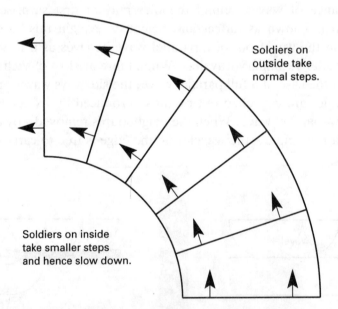

Soldiers on outside take normal steps.

Soldiers on inside take smaller steps and hence slow down.

What has all this got to do with waves? Supposing we think of the wavefront (the line joining the crests of a parallel wave) as being represented by the row of soldiers. The speed with which a wave travels depends upon the medium in which it is travelling. If the wave meets a boundary between two media at an angle, part of the wavefront will be caused to change speed (slow down perhaps) before the others. The effect will be the same as slowing down the left-hand soldiers in the row. The wavefront will execute a left turn or a right turn depending on the angle of approach. This process is called **refraction.**

Superposition and interference

Suppose the wave strikes a wall square on. The reflected wave will pass back towards incoming waves. You could say that there are now two waves travelling in opposite directions on the same stretch of water. Have you ever seen waves striking a sea wall on a rough day? The waves out at sea seem large and menacing. Near to the wall, however, there is a seething cauldron of activity as the height of the water surpasses that of the incoming waves. How can this be? From where does the energy come?

Think about what happens to the surface of the water when a trough from the outgoing wave meets a crest from the incoming one. The poor old water does not know what to do! One wave tries to make it go upwards, and the other tries to make it go down. The net result is that it tries to do both and ends up doing neither. It stays where it is. The two waves are said to have undergone **destructive interference.**

What about the other possibility, when the crest of one wave encounters a crest from another? The water is in no doubt about what to do now – it goes up with a vengeance! The same thing would happen if two troughs were to meet – the water would go down with gusto! This is known as **constructive interference.**

The process of adding the effects of two waves in this way is known as **superposition** and is an important property of all waves.

STATIONARY WAVES

The waves that have been investigated so far have all been what scientists call **progressive** or **travelling waves.** The wave on the water surface near the middle of the lake can be seen to move along. When the wave on the string was described, care was taken to ensure that the string was a long one and that no 'end effects' interfered with the wave.

Another important feature of wave motion is the concept of a **stationary wave.** A stationary wave is really the superposition (combination by adding together) of two waves of identical frequency travelling in opposite directions.

At first, the notion of a 'stationary' wave might seem to be a paradox. How can we talk about a wave if nothing moves along? Care must be taken here to differentiate between the *motion* of the wave (the wave is not a material thing, after all) and the *real change* which takes place in the property of the medium (for example, the height of the water surface in the example we have looked at). Remember, the wave moves along the surface whereas an object floating on the water moves up and down.

Think about the wave that we explored right at the beginning on a tight piece of string. If the string is clamped at both ends, we could be talking about a string on a guitar. The string is plucked so that transverse waves are caused to appear. (We are talking about waves on strings here – not sound waves, which are longitudinal of course.) These waves will move backwards and forwards along the string as they are **reflected** at the fixed ends. As we have already seen, these waves will **interfere** with each other.

Here is a diagram showing three positions of the string with a particular standing wave on it. If you like, it is a series of cine-film frames superimposed on one another. It shows *one* of many possible standing waves that will fit on the string.

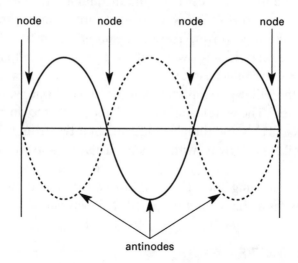

Notice that there are places where the string does not move. We call these places **nodes.** Notice also that there are other places where the amplitude of the oscillation is at a maximum. We call these places **antinodes.** Finally, you should observe that between successive nodes all oscillations are in phase with each other, but they are in antiphase to oscillations in the next inter-node gap.

These arrangements of two waves are called stationary waves because the nodes and antinodes do not move about in space; they remain where they are for all time. Stationary waves are of particular importance in the design of musical instruments, as you will no doubt have gathered!

SOUND

Sound is carried along or **propagated** as a wave. Vibrating objects are sources of sounds. A bell, for example, vibrates when it is struck. Both the metal of the bell and the air inside contribute to this vibration effect. The vibration is transmitted to the air surrounding the bell, and this disturbance is propagated through the air. Sounds can travel through liquids and solids as well as gases. However, we will restrict our discussion mainly to air.

The bell is, in fact, a rather complex source of vibration due to its shape and the fact that the air inside contributes such a large effect. Instead let's consider a much simpler system – a tuning fork.

The tuning fork is quite simply a fork with two prongs of equal dimensions. When one of the prongs of the fork is struck, the pair are caused to oscillate in such a way that they are alternately splayed out and pushed together. If you have a tuning fork, strike the prongs and then place one tip in a cup of water. The water shows up the vibration really well. Try it and see!

What effect does this vibration have on the air near the fork? As the prongs spread out, they push the adjacent air away. This air in turn pushes the next layer of air away and the push is transmitted throughout the surrounding air. Similarly, when the prongs move together, the adjacent layer of air is pushed by the pressure of the surrounding air so that it moves with the prongs. The effect is just as if the prong were pulling the air with it. This 'pull' is also transmitted through the air surrounding the tuning fork. This diagram shows how the layers of air around the tuning fork are affected by its vibrations.

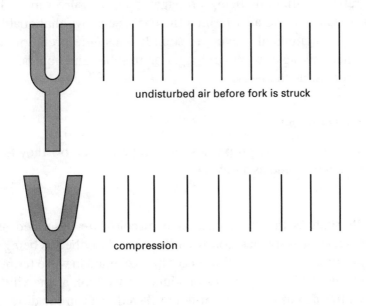

undisturbed air before fork is struck

compression

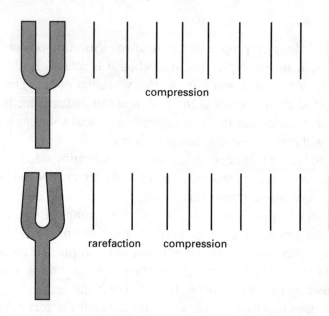

compression

rarefaction   compression

Notice that the layers of air move in a sideways direction, which is also the direction of the propagation of the wave. **Sound is an example of a longitudinal wave.**

Where layers of air are close together, we have what is called a **compression.** In gas terms this means that we have a region of higher than normal pressure. Similarly, where we have layers that are far apart, we have a region which we call a **rarefaction.** When dealing with sound waves it is often more meaningful to talk of pressure variations being propagated as pressure waves. It is the variation in pressure of the air to which the ear is sensitive that enables us to interpret these longitudinal waves as sound. This interpretation is more meaningful when talking of sound propagation in solids and liquids, which are much less compressible than gases.

Wave properties of sound

Now let's have a look at the properties of sound and see how they fit in with our interpretation of sound as a wave.

Pitch

Some sounds, such as the shrill note of a piccolo, are described as 'high' pitched. Others, such as the bass tone of a tuba, are described as being of 'low' pitch. The question is, can these differences be explained in wave terms?

Remember, vibrations are sources of sound. If we look at the vibration of the air caused by each of the different notes played, we can see differences in the **frequency** of the vibrations. Middle C is the musical name for a note which can be found at about the middle of a piano keyboard. (Black notes on a piano come in groups of two and three. C is the first white note on the left of a pair of black notes.) On the scientific or 'just' scale, this note is based on vibrations at 256 oscillations per second. Scientists use the term **hertz** instead of saying 'oscillations per second' all the time. The lowest C on a standard piano keyboard, usually the third white note in from the left, has a fundamental frequency of only 32 hertz. The highest note on a piano is also a C and has a frequency of 4096 hertz.

There is a limit to the range of frequencies that the human hearing system can cope with. The lower limit is difficult to establish, since some low-frequency sounds can be interpreted as a series of fluttering noises. The upper limit varies from person to person, but is usually round about 16,000 hertz (16 kilohertz or kHz for short). Children usually have a higher upper limit than adults. Then again, dogs have a much higher limit to their hearing than humans.

Sounds which are above human hearing are called **ultrasound.** Extremely high-frequency ultrasound is used for medical imaging purposes. In such cases, the sounds travel through the liquid and solid tissues of the body rather than through air.

Loudness

Sound is not all about pitch. Sounds also vary in loudness. The instrument name 'piano' is derived from the term 'pianoforte', meaning literally 'soft-strong' or perhaps 'quiet-loud'. The piano enables the player to make notes sound quiet and gentle, or loud and vigorous.

In wave terms, loudness is associated with the **amplitude** of the sound wave. In terms of pressure, the amplitude refers to the maximum deviation from the ambient or resting pressure. In terms of vibration, amplitude means the maximum distance from the resting position. As you would expect, loud sounds have a larger amplitude of vibration than do quieter sounds. In practice, the relationship is more complicated than simply: the larger the amplitude, the louder the sound.

With musical sounds, loudness is involved in what is known as the **attack** of a note. Instruments like the violin and organ are able to produce notes whose loudness can be sustained at a constant level for some time. Percussion instruments like the xylophone begin very loudly but rapidly suffer a reduction in loudness. This is what we mean by 'attack'.

Reflection

Are there any examples of reflection of sound waves? Of course there are – echoes are reflected sound waves!

Each time a sound wave reaches a boundary, some or all of the wave is reflected. This process is used by bats and submarines. **Sonar** is a process where sounds are generated by the bat or submarine. These sounds then travel outwards until they strike a reflective object. They are then reflected back towards the source. The sender becomes the receiver. By measuring the time it takes for the sound wave to return, the sender can determine how far away the object must be. Information about the reflective properties of the object can also be obtained by noticing how much of the original wave is reflected.

Diffraction

Can sound waves be diffracted? Think about this situation. You are sitting in your favourite armchair relaxing. You just get settled for a well-earned rest when . . . the telephone in the hall rings.

How can you hear the telephone? You are now in one room and the telephone is at the other end of the hall. You have left the door open and the sound of the telephone bell passes through. Even so, you are not in *direct line of sight* of the telephone. This means that the sound wave must have been bent round a corner at the door. What has happened here is that the sound wave was diffracted as it reached the open door. It can therefore be heard anywhere in the room.

Interference

This is not a common feature of sound waves, although it can occur. The reason for this is that sound waves tend to be less regular than, say, waves of light.

The speed of sound

How fast does sound travel? Faster than the waves on the surface of the lake, that's for sure! If this were not the case, you would have to wait for quite a while to hear a friend standing on the other side of the lake calling to you. On the other hand, sound does not travel as fast as light does. If it did, there would not be that gap between seeing the flash of lightning and hearing the sound of the thunder. The reason for the gap is that the light arrives before the sound because it moves much more quickly. So how fast is the speed of sound?

The answer is that it depends. It depends upon what medium the sound is travelling through. For example, it travels much faster through water or solid objects than it does in air. Most often when people ask about the speed of sound they mean in air. Even here it depends on the atmospheric condition at the time. Interestingly though, it does not depend upon the pressure of the air, only the temperature.

In broad terms, the speed of sound in air is of the order of 330 m/sec or 1,200 km/h (over 700 mph in other units). When you think that some aircraft travel at speeds in excess of this, it is really amazing.

Musical sounds

The discussions on waves so far have concentrated on waves of only one frequency, so-called **monochromatic** waves. In reality, most waves consist of many different frequencies all mixed up. The quality of a musical note refers to the purity of the tone. The nearer to monochromatic waves you get, the purer the sound is said to be. The clarinet is an instrument which produces a purer note than, say, a violin.

Music is all about patterns in the sounds. For example, the note called middle C, as we have seen, has a main frequency of 256 Hz. The next highest C has a frequency of 512 Hz. The doubling of the frequency like this is called **moving up by one octave** (CDEFGABC – eight notes).

A pleasing sound may be made up of more than one frequency, but there is still usually a pattern to the mixture. To see how this comes about, we'll look at how musical notes are produced. Let's look at two common types of instrument from the strings and woodwind sections of the orchestra.

Take the stringed instrument first of all. One of the simplest, from a scientific point of view that is, is the guitar. It consists of a series of strings which are stretched over a sound box. To play the instrument, the string is plucked, causing it to vibrate in a special way. To start with, imagine that the string is plucked at the mid-point. We will make the simplifying assumption that the profile of the string as it is plucked is similar to that of the pure wave that we have so far talked about. Notice that the ends of the string are fixed; they are unable to vibrate. The middle of the string is where the vibration has its largest amplitude.

As we have already seen, what we have here is a standing wave. It will be of the simplest type, with *one* antinode in the middle and nodes at each end. At any time the string has half a wavelength sitting on it. (Shortening the string will mean that the half-wavelength and hence the whole wavelength is shorter. Reducing the wavelength of a wave causes its frequency to increase. Thus, shortening the string causes it to oscillate at a higher frequency and therefore a higher pitch. That is how a single guitar string is able to produce its range of notes.)

A skilled guitarist will be able to cause the whole string to vibrate in a different mode. By placing a finger lightly at the middle of the string, plucking it halfway between this and the nut (the end of the string) and rapidly removing the finger, the string can be made to vibrate with a node in the middle as well as each end. This is the example we saw earlier in the section on stationary waves. This mode of vibration has *two* antinodes. Now a whole wavelength fits on the string. This causes the wavelength to be halved, which causes the frequency to be doubled. The same length of string is able to vibrate at a higher frequency.

It is also possible for the string to vibrate with three antinodes. In fact, any wave organized such that a whole number of half-wavelengths fits on the length of the string will cause the string to vibrate in yet another mode.

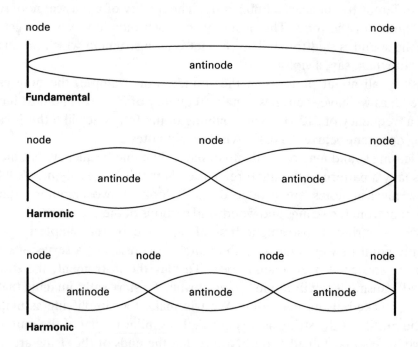

The first mode, the one with only one antinode in the middle, is called the **fundamental.** This produces the main note of the instrument. The other modes are called **harmonics** or **overtones.** A pure note will consist of only the fundamental with no overtones. The quality of the note is determined by the strength and number of harmonics. A perfect-quality note has no harmonics, only the fundamental.

When a guitar string is plucked, some of the harmonics are sounded as well as the fundamental. The musical note that is heard is the fundamental, but the harmonics lend the guitar its distinctive sound.

A similar kind of process occurs in the case of wind instruments. Instead of a string vibrating, a column of air in a pipe is used. Let's consider a pipe which is open at one end and closed at the other. The air in the tube can be set oscillating by blowing across the top. You may have tried this already, by blowing across the top of a bottle to produce a sound.

The air is free to vibrate at the top, so this will be an antinode. The air at the bottom is prevented from oscillating by the closure. This end will be a node. The fundamental note is sounded when the first antinode is at the top of the tube. The length of the tube will be one-quarter wavelength in this case. The first harmonic is formed when there is another antinode below the one at the top, as shown in the diagram.

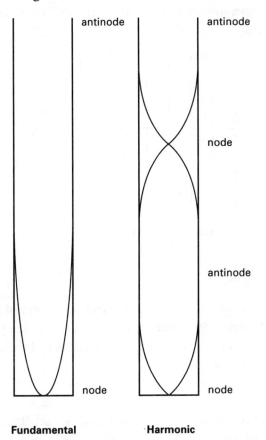

As you can see, changing the length of the pipe will change the frequency or pitch of the note produced. Changing the number and relative strengths of the harmonics will change the quality of the note.

Please note: This diagram makes it easy to see the nodes and antinodes, but it does have one significant drawback. In order to make it clear, it represents the wave as transverse (a sound wave in air is longitudinal, remember). The air in the tube oscillates in a vertical direction, not horizontally as the diagram seems to suggest.

LIGHT

Rays

Before embarking on a detailed study of the topic of light, something needs to be said about rays. It might seem at first that the idea of a ray and the idea of a wave are not compatible. In fact this is not the case.

Think for a moment of a beam of light in terms of a wavefront steadily advancing through space. Imagine a point on that wavefront advancing steadily forwards. If you were to draw a line in space tracing the path of this point, you would have drawn in a ray. Rays then will always be drawn at right angles to wavefronts.

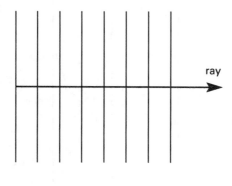

advancing wavefronts

Wave properties of light

You have no doubt often heard it said that light is a form of wave. You should now know enough about the properties of waves to make your own mind up about this, based on certain information. In order to be classified as a wave, light must behave in certain ways.

Reflection

Anyone who has ever looked in a mirror knows that light can be reflected. Think about a ray of light as it strikes a mirror. There will be *one* such ray that will strike the mirror and be reflected back along the way it came. This ray has followed a line called the **normal.** The normal can also be thought of as a line at right angles to the mirror's surface. The angle between the incoming or **incident** ray and this normal is called the **angle of incidence.** The angle between the reflected ray and the normal is called the **angle of reflection.**

One of the so-called laws of reflection says that **the angle of incidence equals the angle of reflection.** This is in agreement with the idea of reflection already discussed. Remember that the angle between the incoming wave and the wall (the reflecting surface) was equal to the angle between the reflected wave and the wall (angles A and B in the diagram on page 130).

Refraction

Light can also be refracted. It is not commonly known that the speed of light is much faster in a vacuum than through glass or water, for example. In water it is three-quarters and in glass it is two-thirds of the speed in a vacuum. The speed of light in air differs little from the vacuum speed. **This variation in speed means that light can be refracted as it passes from air into glass or water.**

Consider a ray of light passing from air into a glass block with a flat surface, as shown in the diagram.

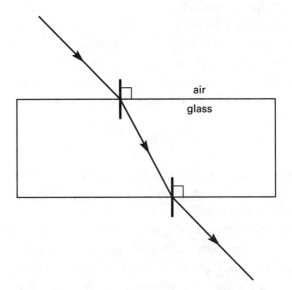

air

glass

A **normal** has been drawn at right angles to the surface of the glass. The path of the ray through the block can be seen. You should notice that, as it passes from the air to the block, it is bent towards the normal. Notice also that, as it leaves the block, it is bent away from the normal. The deviation is the same in each case so that, as the ray emerges, it is parallel to, though offset from, the ray that entered the block.

Refraction is a very important property of light. Lenses work on this principle. Without refraction not only would optical instruments fail to work, but our eyes would be unable to uses lenses to help us see.

Diffraction

We have always been told that light travels in a straight line . . . but does it? Light *can* be diffracted, although it is not often that you can see round corners in the same way that you can hear round corners!

The effects of diffraction are not readily apparent in an everyday sense. If you go to buy a pair of binoculars, you will find that they come with a number of different specifications. One specification is the magnification. A second specification is a little more mysterious. It is the diameter of the objective lens. This is the lens at the front that gathers the light. Why should this be important?

To be sure, it does have an effect on the amount of light that the instrument can gather, but that is not all by any means. The objective lens forms an opening at the front of the binoculars which causes diffraction. It is, after all, a gap surrounded by barriers just like a gap in a pier through which water waves may be diffracted. The light is diffracted at the barrier. This affects the resolving power of the binoculars.

A picture with poor resolution is fuzzy. It cannot be put into sharper focus. The limit to the clarity depends upon the diameter of the objective lens. The larger the lens, the clearer the image can be. A pair of binoculars with good resolving power will be able to distinguish two objects as separate at distances at which a pair with inferior resolving power would make them appear as a single larger blob.

Interference

Have you ever wondered why it is that rain puddles on an oily road manage to have such beautiful coloured streaks on the surface? The property of *interference of light* is responsible for this effect.

The oil floats on the surface of the water of the puddle. Usually this is only a very thin film of oil. White light, as we will see, is made up of all the colours of the rainbow mixed together. When it strikes the surface of the oil, some of the light is reflected and most is transmitted through the oil. When this transmitted light strikes the water surface, some of it is reflected as well. This means that there are now *two* rays reflected from the film, one from the top and one from the bottom. Remember that a ray is only the path of a point on an advancing wavefront. The two rays come originally from the same wavefront as each other. The one that was reflected from the bottom surface has had to travel just a little further than the other.

Imagine two trains, with alternate black and white trucks, running on parallel tracks in the same direction. The black trucks of the train may represent peaks, while the white trucks may represent troughs. Scientists even talk of 'wave trains'! If the two trains are level, white trucks will always line up with white, and black will match with black. This will give **constructive interference.** What if one of the trains is exactly one truck length behind the other? Now trucks of opposite colour will be lined up. You could say that they are out of phase. A peak will line up with a trough and vice versa on the wave train. This is known as **destructive interference.**

As you will soon see, light of different wavelengths appears as different colours. White light is a mixture of all visible wavelengths. If the two wavefronts of one particular colour from a beam of multi-coloured white light reflected from the oil film are separated by a distance of half a wavelength, they will be out of phase and the interference will be destructive. This destructive interference will cancel some of the wavelengths and therefore colours from the full spectrum of white light. If some of the colours have been removed, the others will remain. The reflection will no longer be white, but a beautiful multi-coloured pattern.

Electromagnetic waves

So, are you convinced that light is a form of wave? Good, but what exactly *is* the disturbance that is transmitted as a wave in this case? The fact that light can travel through a vacuum means that there is nothing material to vibrate, as there is in the case of sound waves. Instead there is a transmission of electric and magnetic disturbances, which is why light is described as being an example of **electromagnetic waves.**

Polarization

Light is a transverse wave. Go back to thinking about another transverse wave, a wave on a string. Imagine that this string passes through a card with a slot in it. If the slot is arranged so that it runs vertically, it constrains the string to oscillate in a vertical direction. Horizontal waves will be unable to pass through. Only vertical waves will be allowed on the string the other side of the slot. We call this process **plane polarization.** We can, of course, orientate the slot in any direction we like. However, it is not possible to polarize longitudinal waves in this way. Think about it!

Light can be polarized. You will have heard of Polaroid sunglasses. Perhaps you know that if the lenses from two pairs of glasses are held one in front of the other and one is rotated, the pair of lenses can be made to go more or less completely black. This is what would happen if you had two cards with slots in held at right angles to each other, and tried to pass a wave on a string through the combination. The first card lets waves polarized in one direction through, but the other will not allow these waves to pass. The result is that no waves pass.

The electromagnetic spectrum

Electromagnetic waves can have a wide variety of frequencies. The lowest frequencies are called **radio waves.** A look at any standard radio receiver will show you that radio waves are classified with terms such as 'long wave', 'medium wave' and 'short wave'. FM radio is classified as 'very high frequency' or VHF. Television uses 'ultra high frequency' radio waves, or UHF.

At the next highest frequencies above radio waves come **microwaves.** Microwaves are well known for their kitchen application in ovens. When absorbed by water molecules, they have the effect of causing heating. It is not so well known that microwaves are the radiation used in radar. Microwaves are emitted by the radar station, reflected by the target and then detected by the dish back at the station. The process is very similar to sonar used by submarines. Radar has a longer range than sonar. Modern defence needs have made radar technology very advanced indeed.

Next comes **infra-red**, which is better known as radiant heat. This is because hot bodies emit infra-red. The effect that infra-red radiation has when it is absorbed is to cause heating. Cooking appliances that claim to be infra-red are really only using radiant heat, which even camp fires produce! Do not be put off by scientific jargon. Infra-red is the radiation which is sought by firemen using detectors to find victims buried under rubble during disasters. All warm, living bodies are at a temperature above the surroundings and so emit infra-red radiation.

The visible part of the spectrum, which we call 'light' is formed by only a very narrow frequency band. We will discuss the visible part of the spectrum in more detail presently.

After this comes **ultraviolet (UV)**, which is responsible for sunburn. Ultraviolet waves are in fact a harmful form of radiation. The Sun gives off a great deal of UV radiation. Fortunately, before this arrives at the surface of the Earth much of it is absorbed by a layer of **ozone** in the upper atmosphere. This layer appears to be in danger at the moment due to atmospheric pollution caused by CFC gases. Many people make the mistake of confusing this ozone layer depletion problem with global warming. Global warming is caused by a build-up of carbon dioxide in the atmosphere, and has nothing to do with UV or ozone.

X-rays are next. There is quite a range of frequencies for X-rays. X-rays are dangerous radiation. Their use in hospitals for both diagnostic and therapeutic purposes is now carefully controlled. A specially trained member of staff, the radiographer, is responsible for ensuring the safe use of X-rays.

Finally, at the highest frequency of all, we have **gamma rays.** It is the gamma radiation that most people know of as 'radiation' in the context of nuclear power stations and nuclear weapons.

The visible part of the spectrum

Just what makes blue light blue? The various colours of light are really only electromagnetic waves of different frequencies. At the lower-frequency end of the visible part of the spectrum is red light. You may have already guessed this, as it is next to infra-red. The colours of the rainbow in order of increasing frequency are as follows:

red   orange   yellow   green   blue   indigo   violet

Violet is the last visible colour before ultraviolet.

What about white and black? White light is simply a mixture of light of all of the visible frequencies. Black, on the other hand, is an absence of visible light at all.

Rainbows are useful as a lead in to discussions of white light. White light from the Sun contains all the colours of the rainbow. When sunshine strikes droplets of water in the atmosphere it is split up, in this instance by differential refraction, into its constituent colours. This type of process is called **dispersion.** You can create an artificial rainbow of your own using a glass prism. If you shine a beam of white light from a lamp so that it strikes the surface of a prism at the correct angle, the light that emerges will have been dispersed. The following diagram shows how this is done.

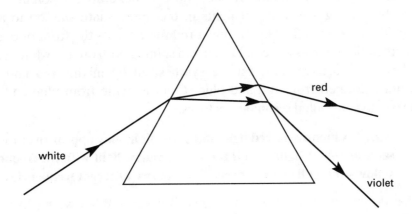

This works because the speed at which light passes through glass depends upon the frequency. Violet light moves more slowly in glass than red light does. This means that violet light is bent more by refraction than red.

There are many other colours which can be seen besides those of the rainbow. To learn more about how we 'see' colour, it is necessary to examine the way that the eye detects different colours.

The eye contains two types of light-sensitive cell. **Rod cells**, the first type, are not able to differentiate colour, but are sensitive to low light levels. In semi-dark conditions it is the rods that respond. That is why you cannot distinguish colours in very dim conditions. The other light-sensitive cells are called **cone cells.** We do not have receptors for each of the possible colours. There are only three types of cone. Some are sensitive mainly to red light, some mainly to green light and the others mainly to blue.

If an object emits or reflects red light, it will stimulate the red cones and we will see red. We see green and blue in a similar way.

Yellow light will be of a frequency which is able to stimulate both the green- and red-sensitive cones together. If both sets of cones are stimulated, we see yellow. We can be deceived into seeing yellow by stimulating the red cones with red light at the same time as stimulating the green cones with green light. This is how we are able to see yellow on a colour TV set. TV screens are covered in patches of three different kinds of phosphor, some of which will emit red light, some green and some blue. **We are deceived into seeing colours that are not there by having the right set of phosphors radiate the appropriate mix of colours to our eyes.**

Remember, the eye is only *one* organ of vision. The other important organ is, of course, the brain. The brain also has a marked effect on how we see colour.

As a result of the eye mechanism described above, scientists call red, green and blue the **primary colours.** In fact you can make up any colour that you care to by shining a mixture of lights in the appropriate way on to a white screen. Try making yellow by placing a red filter across the front of one torch and a green filter across a second torch and shining both on to a white screen.

Yellow, as we have said, can be synthesized by mixing red and green. Magenta is formed from red and blue. Cyan is made from blue and green. These colours are called **secondary colours.**

N.B.   A mixture of red light and green light may appear to our eyes the same as yellow light. But it is not true yellow light with the frequency of yellow – it is still red and green lights of two different frequencies.

What do we mean when we say 'Grass is green'? What we mean is that if you shine white light on to grass, it will absorb light other than green which it will reflect. We see only the reflected green light, so we say 'Grass is green'.

In art lessons, the primary colours are red, yellow and blue. Why is this? **When you mix colours in art what you are doing is mixing paints not lights.**

Let's look at why it is that mixing yellow and blue paints makes green.

Yellow paint contains pigment that reflects red, yellow and green lights, but absorbs blue. This will make the eye see yellow. Blue paint contains pigments that reflects blue and green light, but absorbs red and yellow. You interpret this as blue. When you put the two together, the blue pigment absorbs the red and yellow, the yellow pigment absorbs the blue. All you are left with is green!

REVIEW

Let's reflect upon what we have found out. We have looked at many different phenomena from wiggling strings to beams of coloured light. Although they are different, they all have certain features in common. Because of these common features we decide to recognize them by their shared characteristics. This is what we now call wave motion. All waves transfer energy from one place to another. The term 'wave' refers to a type of behaviour. We are better able to say what waves *do* rather than what they *are!*

Chapter 6

The Earth and Space

INTRODUCTION

Children often hold quite different views of the nature of the Earth and space from the accepted 'scientific' explanations. Many children 'know' that the Earth is round, because they have been told that this is the case. But their common sense tells them that the Earth is flat. How do they come to terms with this apparent contradiction? Children can be very inventive in this area. They keep the internalization of a flat Earth, but try to account for the roundness.

Some of these strategies involve thinking of the roundness in *two dimensions only*. The Earth is like a round island in the middle of a surrounding ocean. To circumnavigate the Earth is to sail round the island, just like the Round Britain race. Alternatively, the roundness is accounted for by the rounded tops of hills or other geographic features.

Some children are aware of the third dimension. They appreciate the sphericity of the Earth. Strangely, this can still be reconciled with flatness. Imagine that you have a large water melon. Take a machette and chop through the fruit. Suppose you are left with two unequal parts. Take the larger part and lay it on the ground, round side down. It will right itself until the slice is uppermost. Look carefully at the slice. It forms a flat surface. Imagine that the removed part of the fruit is replaced with 'atmosphere' and you have a round model of the Earth with a flat surface on which to live!

Other children are fully aware that the Earth we inhabit is a globe, and that we all live on the surface. However, they have not yet managed to come to terms with notions of 'up' and 'down'.

If you draw an image of the Earth on a piece of paper, children will recognize that a person standing on the Earth will have two feet firmly attached to the ground, but 'up' and 'down' follow the edges of the paper. 'Up' and 'down' are *external* to the Earth. Pouring out a fizzy drink becomes a curious experience as you progress round the globe.

Then again, other children have grasped the idea of a spherical Earth with gravity acting at right angles to the surface. However, they have not yet managed to understand how 'up' and 'down' can be described *beneath* the surface. For them, a vertical mine shaft is not one that goes to the centre of the Earth but is relative to something external.

Finally, some have reached the scientifically accepted view of a spherical Earth with people living on the surface and 'up' and 'down' being ideas which operate radially from the centre of the globe.

THE MOON

The Moon is our nearest neighbour in space. It is a giant lump of rock some 1,350 km or so across and just under 150,000 km away on average. The expression 'on average' is used because the Moon does not form a circular orbit around the Earth, but an ellipse or squashed circle.

The curious thing about the way that the Moon orbits the Earth is that it takes the same time to complete one orbit, about 27 days, as it takes to revolve once about its own axis. This means that it always presents the same face to the Earth.

The shape of the illuminated portion of the Moon, as seen from the Earth, changes from day to day. We talk about the **phases of the Moon**.

The diagram on page 152 shows how the Moon appears from an observation point on the northern hemisphere of the Earth. If you are in the southern hemisphere, when at A the Moon will appear as shown in view G, at B it will look like view F, and so on.

The surface of the Moon does not have its own source of light. We rely on reflected sunlight to see the Moon. One-half of the Moon is always bathed in sunlight whilst the other is in deep shadow. Naturally, the bright half is the one facing the Sun. As you can see from the diagram, we see the Moon from an angle. The angle changes as the Moon orbits the Earth. We always see the same face of the Moon whether it is in shadow or sunshine. When part of the Moon that is facing us is in sunlight, we see only that part.

Occasionally, the Moon comes directly between the Sun and the Earth. When it does so, it casts a shadow on the Earth. This is called an **eclipse of the Sun**. Although the Sun is much larger than the Moon, it is much further away.

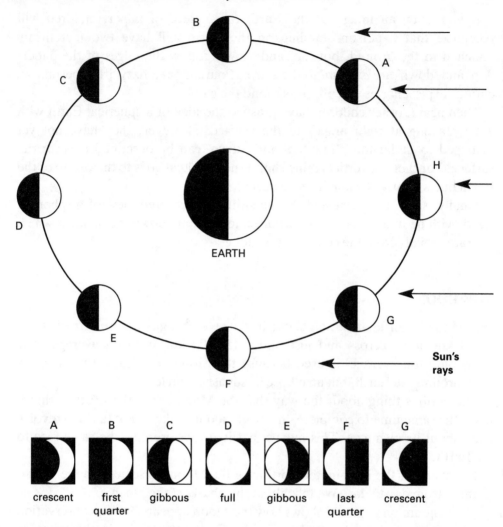

View of the Moon as seen from the northern hemisphere. (View would be in reverse order from the southern hemisphere.)

The result is that, by coincidence, the Moon appears to us to take up the same amount of sky as the Sun. This means that the Moon is able to blot out the Sun completely during a total eclipse.

More frequently, because of the larger size of the Earth, the Moon passes through the Earth's shadow. When this happens we see an **eclipse of the Moon**. During the space of a few hours the Moon appears to have a bite taken out of it as the Earth's shadow passes across the face.

During the time when it is in complete shadow, the Moon appears red to us from the Earth. The few rays of the Sun that *do* manage to reach the Moon have had to pass through the Earth's atmosphere. We see such rays from the Sun during the early morning and late evening. You will no doubt have noticed the characteristic red glow. The blue light is scattered by the atmospheric dust more that the red light. It is this red light that illuminates the Moon during an eclipse. Incidentally, the scattering of the blue light in this way gives the open sky its characteristic blue colour.

To a large extent, the tides here on Earth are influenced by the Moon. The water in the seas of the Earth is attracted to heavenly bodies like the Sun and the Moon by the force of gravity. The Moon has a large influence because it is the nearest. As the Earth rotates, the Moon changes its position relative to the oceans and causes the direction of the gravitational pull to change. This causes the tidal effects that we see.

When the Moon is low down in the sky, it may appear flattened and reddish. This is due to the large thickness of atmosphere through which the light has to pass. The atmosphere acts as a sort of lens and distorts the apparent shape of the Moon.

DAY AND NIGHT

During the day, in the absence of cloud, the Sun shines down on us from the sky. At night the Sun cannot be seen. It is surprising the confusion that the mechanism of day and night causes in the minds of children. Suggestions such as 'The Sun goes to sleep at night' or 'The Sun goes behind a cloud' are often heard. The idea of the part of the Earth on which they sit facing away from the Sun seems difficult to grasp. They are not always aware that it is day-time in some parts of the world when it is night-time in others.

Even some adults are confused by time differences. At any instant in time that you are to mention, there is a place on the Earth's surface where the rays from the Sun fall vertically downwards. The local time at that place on the Earth is noon. At that instant, any point on the surface of the Earth along a line from pole to pole passing through that place will find the Sun at its highest point in the sky for that day, and therefore also has local noon. In practice, it would be very difficult if 12 noon on the clocks were allowed to differ minute by minute as you passed through a country from east to west. For this reason, 'clock time' is standardized into various zones differing from each other by one hour. Time differences occur if you travel in an easterly or westerly direction, but not if you travel north or south. If you travel west, you will find that you have to put your clock back. Conversely, if you travel east, you put your clock forward.

Sometimes governments of countries decide to operate on a different time scale from each other, so that UK time differs from French time by an hour or so depending on the time of year. This is done by agreement, not by scientific necessity.

SEASONS

How do seasons happen? For our purposes we can consider that the Earth spins on its axis once every day. As far as the seasons are concerned, the important thing is that the axis of the Earth's orbit is not perpendicular to the plane of its orbit. Rather it is tilted an angle of 23 degrees or so. Look at the following diagram to get an idea of what this means.

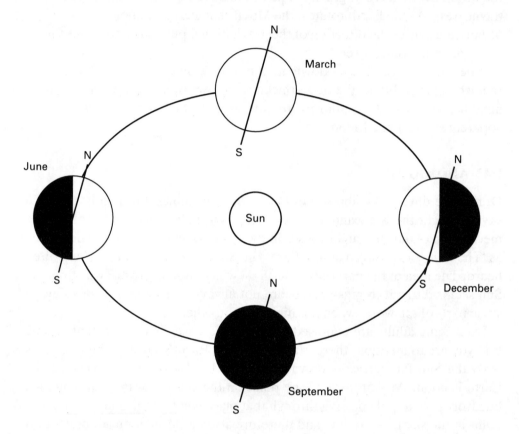

View of Earth's orbit as seen from a point slightly above the plane of the orbit

Notice that in December the North Pole is tilted away from the Sun, while the South Pole is tilted towards it. In June the reverse happens. During March and September the tilt is sideways on to the Sun and neither pole is tilted towards or away from it. Seasons become more noticeably different the nearer you get to the poles. On the other hand, if you live on the equator or in the tropics, the notion of winter or summer has little meaning. Shifting wind patterns that may bring about dry and rainy seasons become more significant.

In more temperate regions, the seasons are summer, autumn, winter and spring, although of course when it is winter in the northern hemisphere (north of the equator) it is summer in the southern hemisphere, and vice versa. Similarly, spring in the north is at the same time as autumn in the south.

Just how does tilting affect the season? By the sound of it, being tilted towards the Sun could mean that one pole is nearer to the Sun than the other. But it is not as simple as mere proximity to the Sun. The Sun is so far away that the small distance involved is insignificant. No, there are more subtle changes at work.

This diagram shows a view of the Earth during summer in the northern hemisphere. The two points A and B are chosen such that the distance from A to the North Pole is the same as the distance from B to the South Pole. Also the two points are on the same line of longitude, a line joining the two poles.

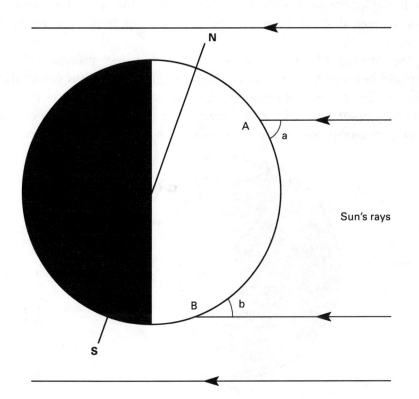

Notice the angles *a* and *b*. These indicate the angle that the Sun's rays make with the surface of the Earth at the two points. At A the angle is large, meaning that the Sun is high in the sky. In contrast, at B the angle is small and the Sun appears close to the horizon. This means the Sun's rays are stronger at A in the summer than they are at B in the winter.

To understand this better, look at the next diagram. It shows two sunbeams of equal width *d* shining down on a portion of the Earth. One is at a high angle, the other is at a low angle.

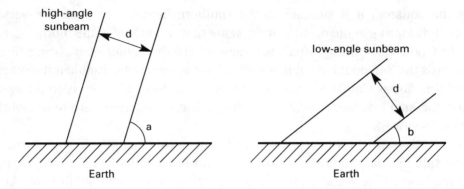

Notice how much more of the Earth the low-angle beam has to illuminate. The high-angle sunbeam is more concentrated. Clearly, the low-angle beam has had to pass through more energy-scattering atmosphere than the high-angle beam.

So the heating effect of the Sun's rays is more pronounced in the hemisphere in which the pole is tilted towards the Sun. That is not all though. The first of the next pair of diagrams shows a view of the Earth as it would be seen from a point vertically above where the terminator (the line between light and dark) most closely approaches the North Pole in midsummer.

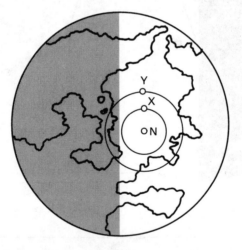

View of the Arctic Circle in summer

The North Pole has been marked in as N. The circles represent the paths traced out by points X and Y as the Earth rotates about its axis. Notice that point X never passes into the dark side of the Earth. It is always in sunlight. Point X would have to be north of the Arctic Circle, the land of the midnight Sun. Even at point Y you will notice that it spends a greater part of the circle and therefore a greater part of the day in the daylight. That is why in summer the nights are short and the days are long.

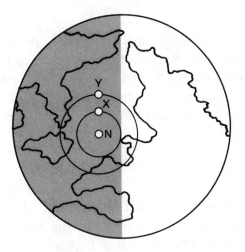

View of the Arctic Circle in winter

During the winter notice that point X above the Arctic Circle never passes into the daylight. The Sun never appears above the horizon. Even at Y the day is very short and the night is long.

During the spring and summer equinox (literally, equal days and equal nights) the terminator passes through the North and South Poles, so we get half of the day in daylight and the other half in the dark.

In summary, then, in winter the Sun's rays are weak and the time that the Sun can shine is short. In summer the Sun's rays are more concentrated and the period of daylight is longer. The combination of these two factors is responsible for what we call the seasons.

THE PLANETS

There are nine known planets in orbit around our Sun. In order of increasing distance from the Sun they are Mercury, Venus, Earth, Mars, Jupiter, Saturn, Uranus, Neptune and Pluto. Pluto's orbit is slightly odd and there are occasions when it is closer to the Sun than Neptune, although Neptune never reaches the distance of furthest approach that Pluto does. One interesting feature of the planets in what is described as the **solar system** is that they all orbit the Sun in the same plane. That is to say, you can visualize their orbits as if they all went round on a giant plate with the Sun almost at the centre.

Mercury

Mercury is not often visible because it is very close to the Sun and is lost in the Sun's glare as a consequence. Sometimes, however, it can appear low on the horizon just after sunset, looking like an evening star. Not only is Mercury the nearest planet to the Sun, it is also the smallest planet, being only three-eighths of the diameter of the Earth. Mercury has no atmosphere and is not much more than a barren rock.

Venus

Venus is roughly the same size as the planet Earth. It is surrounded by a densely clouded atmosphere. The surface of the planet is very hot, 480 °Celsius or so on the sunlit side and still as high as 370 °Celsius on the dark side. The fact that Venus is inside the Earth's orbit means that, when viewed from the Earth, it can be seen to have phases like the Moon. Venus is the brightest planet and can often be seen in the day-time.

Earth

Our home planet. Since the beginnings of space exploration, the nature of our world as a planet in orbit around the Sun has been brought home to us by the startling pictures that have been obtained. The effect has been a humbling one.

Mars

The so-called Red Planet. Surface features of Mars can be seen through a large telescope. The white polar icecaps can be seen to shrink and grow with the Martian seasons. It is thought that the 'ice' formed there is really mainly frozen carbon dioxide. Recent unmanned landings on Mars have found that the planet has an atmosphere, shown by the light sky, but that the atmosphere is very thin. It is thought highly improbable that Mars is capable of supporting life. The surface of Mars is cratered like our Moon. Mars, like the Earth, is not alone in its orbit. It has two small satellites or moons named Deimos and Phobos.

The asteroid belt

Mention is made here of the asteroid belt, which is a region between the orbits of Mars and the next planet, Jupiter, containing huge numbers of chunks of rock called **asteroids**. These rocks vary in size from a few kilometres to several hundred kilometres across. It is thought that the asteroid belt could be the remains of a former planet that was somehow destroyed.

Jupiter

Jupiter is the largest planet of the solar system. Its mass is over three hundred times that of the Earth. The atmosphere of Jupiter appears as a series of belts from the Earth. Many storms can be seen going on. Of particular interest is a giant storm called the Red Spot. The atmosphere is mainly hydrogen, methane and ammonia, and is thought to be hundreds of miles deep. Like Mars, Jupiter has moons, twelve in all, the largest of which resemble minor planets.

Saturn

Saturn is well known as the ringed planet. It is the second largest of our planets, a giant ball of ice surrounded by frozen clouds which, like Jupiter's, form into bands. The atmosphere is similar to that of Jupiter, but with more methane and less ammonia. Saturn has many moons, nine of which are named. One moon, Titan, is so large that it even has its own atmosphere.

Uranus

Uranus is the third largest planet. It is so far from the Sun, over 19 times as far as the Earth, that it takes 84 Earth years to complete one orbit. It is now known that Uranus also has a ring system, though less dramatic than that of Saturn. One strange feature of the planet is the axis of its rotation. Uranus seems to lie on its side, as it were, with its equator almost at right angles to its orbit.

Neptune

Neptune was not discovered until 1846. It is over 30 times as far from the Sun as the Earth. It takes almost 165 of our years to complete one orbit.

Pluto

Pluto takes 248 Earth years to complete one orbit. Its mass is just over half that of the Earth. It is not known whether Pluto is the last planet of the solar system. Astronomers disagree as to the likelihood of there being more.

THE SUN

So far we have discussed the nine known planets of our solar system, but we have not really talked about the 'star performer', the Sun!

Certainly, in more ways than one the Sun occupies centre stage in the solar system. It provides the source of energy which enables life to exist on Earth. It provides the light for us to see the other members of the solar system by reflection. It is the most massive of the bodies within the solar system. So large is it that, if you placed the Earth at the centre of the Sun, the Moon would orbit roughly halfway between the Earth and the surface of the Sun.

How did the Sun come about? What makes the Sun glow so brightly? What is it that makes it work? These are just some of the questions that need to be answered in order to understand our place in the universe.

To start off with, there is nothing special about our Sun. It is just one of countless millions of stars in the Universe. It is not even very remarkable as stars go. What makes it so special to us is its proximity. Our Sun is the nearest star.

Just what is the Sun then? It is a ball of what scientists call **plasma**. A plasma is like a gas made of atoms with the electrons stripped off. The Sun is made of a plasma of hydrogen with some helium and a small mixture of other elements. All this material is held together by the Sun's enormous gravity. It obtains its supply of energy by transmuting hydrogen into helium by nuclear fusion. The Sun is a giant nuclear fusion reactor.

THE STARS

The Sun is the nearest star to Earth, but it is still about 150 million kilometres away. It takes light a little over eight minutes to reach us from the Sun. The next nearest star is much further away. It is so far away that it takes light about four *years* to make the journey. Such a star is said to be four light-years away. A *light-year* is the distance that light will travel in one year. It is a measure of *distance* and not *time*, as many people seem to think.

Stars come in many different sizes, colours and temperatures. Some stars turn out to be **double stars** when viewed through a telescope. Double stars rotate about a common axis and belong to the same star system.

The largest stars are called **red giants.** These are so large that they could swallow up the entire Earth's orbit and still have room to spare. The material from which they are made, however, is very diffuse; so much so that on Earth we would say that it is almost a vacuum!

At the other end of things there are **white dwarfs.** A matchbox of material forming a white dwarf would have a mass of several tonnes.

Our Sun, in common with many stars, began as a cool cloud of interstellar gas and dust. This cloud collapsed under the force of its own gravity. As it collapsed, its temperature increased until eventually it became hot enough for nuclear fusion to take place. A star was born. The new star was destined to occupy a stable state for many millions of years.

Strangely enough, the larger the mass of the star, the shorter the time it sustains its period of relative stability. But how the star ends up depends upon many other factors too. As far as our own Sun is concerned, at the end of its period of stability its core is expected to shrink and its outer layers will expand to fill a much larger volume. The Sun will become a red giant and the Earth will be swallowed up. Red giants sooner or later reach an unstable stage where it is quite possible for them suddenly to flare up as novae. This may happen several times to any given star.

When all the nuclear fuel of the star has been used up, it continues to collapse under its own gravity. The star may turn into a white dwarf, which will continue to radiate its energy away until it becomes a dead dark star. It is thought that more massive stars may blow themselves apart as supernovae, leaving a dark neutron star at the centre. Either way, the prospect for all stars is a grim one! We need not worry, though, because all this will happen in the far distant future, thousands of millions of years ahead!

CONSTELLATIONS

At first glance, to the untrained eye, the night sky looks to be a confusing mass of stars randomly painted against a dark backdrop. Anyone contemplating making astronomical observations needs to have some reference points from which to start.

In ancient times, certain patterns in the sky were noticed and related to mythical figures. Such groupings are called the **constellations.** However, although two stars may be found in the same constellation, this does not imply that they are near to one another. The groupings within the constellations relate only to how they *appear* from Earth.

For example, the brightest star in the constellation Orion is called Betelgeuse and is a red star about 520 light-years distant. The next brightest, called Rigel, is 900 light-years away. Rigel must be of similar distance to Betelgeuse as Betelgeuse is to Earth.

Constellations are extremely valuable pointers to which part of the sky you are looking at. One star that it might be useful to be able to locate is Polaris, the pole star. This star appears nearly vertically above the North Pole. If you can find it in the sky then you can find the direction north. This is one simple way that you can navigate using the stars. To find one star is difficult, but to find the constellation called the Plough is much easier. You will find that the last two stars of the Plough, Merak and Dubhe, can be used as a pointer to Polaris.

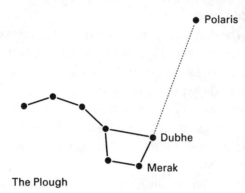

The Plough

Once you can recognize the Plough, you can find Polaris. In the southern hemisphere, the Southern Cross constellation is used to locate south.

STARS AND GALAXIES

Not all of the bright objects that you can see in the night sky are stars or planets. Some objects do not simply appear as dots of light, as stars do. Some appear as faint smudges. These smudges are called **nebulae** (singular, **nebula**). Some nebulae are clouds of gas. Others are views of distant galaxies. The great distance of these galaxies makes it impossible to resolve individual stars, which is why they appear as misty smudges.

In the constellation of Andromeda is a nebula called M31. This is shown up by telescopes to be spiral-shaped. It turns out to be one and a half *million* light-years away. This means that it takes light one and a half million years to reach us from M31. You are really looking at how it appeared that long ago, not as it really is now! M31 is 120,000 light-years across. Astronomers call this object a **spiral galaxy.** A galaxy is a collection of stars. Our own galaxy is thought to be a spiral galaxy similar to M31.

You can often see a milky-white luminescence stretching right across the bright sky. This is called the **Milky Way.** What you are looking at is the centre of your own galaxy. These stars are so distant and so dense that they appear as a dim glow through the sky; you cannot make out individual stars. We live in a typical spiral-shaped galaxy. There are other galaxies in space which are not like ours, but which are elliptical or even shapeless.

THE UNIVERSE

The science of cosmology is the study of the nature of space, time and matter in what we call the **universe.** The universe is really another way of saying 'everything that exists'. The kind of questions asked are, 'what is it? and where did it come from?

To begin with, space is *not* infinitely large. You cannot keep going on for ever and ever without reaching the end. Space is not just an empty place in which the universe has been placed. Space is part of the fabric of the universe, so it cannot exist without the matter in it.

Modern theories of the origin of the universe talk of a 'big bang'. It is thought that, at the earliest time in the universe, everything was compressed to a tiny point. It rapidly expanded from there to the present day. Observations show that the universe is constantly in a state of expansion and that, the further away you look from where you are, the greater the rate of expansion becomes. This is consistent with a big-bang theory. We cannot say anything about what happened before the big bang, since things were so chaotic then as to destroy any evidence of what went before, if anything!

In order to think about how it will all end, we need to look back to the study of energy. In particular, remember that for anything to happen energy needs to be transferred. Where does the energy go to? It ends up as low-grade heat. This paints a dismal picture of the 'heat death of the universe'. It means that all the energy will eventually become dissipated more and more widely. The universe, as it grows ever larger, could be said to be doomed as it eventually cools off.

Index